First World War
and Army of Occupation
War Diary
France, Belgium and Germany

25 DIVISION
7 Infantry Brigade
Manchester Regiment
21st Battalion
1 September 1918 - 5 July 1919

WO95/2244/5

The Naval & Military Press Ltd
www.nmarchive.com
Published in association with The National Archives

Published by

The Naval & Military Press Ltd

Unit 10 Ridgewood Industrial Park,

Uckfield, East Sussex,

TN22 5QE England

Tel: +44 (0) 1825 749494

www.naval-military-press.com

www.nmarchive.com

This diary has been reprinted in facsimile from the original. Any imperfections are inevitably reproduced and the quality may fall short of modern type and cartographic standards.

© Crown Copyright
Images reproduced by permission of The National Archives, London, England, 2015.

Contents

Document type	Place/Title	Date From	Date To
Heading	WO95/2244-5		
Heading	7 Bde In Gun Coy Feb Vol 2		
Heading	21st Bn Manchester Regt Sept 1918-Jly 1919 From Italy 7 Div. 91 Bde		
War Diary	Arzignano	01/09/1918	12/09/1918
War Diary	On The Train	13/09/1918	16/09/1918
War Diary	Neuilly-L'Hopital	17/09/1918	25/09/1918
War Diary	Neuilly L'Hopital	26/09/1918	26/09/1918
War Diary	On the Train	27/09/1918	27/09/1918
War Diary	Franvillers	28/09/1918	28/09/1918
War Diary	Montauban (Trow Wood)	29/09/1918	30/09/1918
Operation(al) Order(s)	21st (S) Battalion The Manchester Regiment Operation Order No. 152	12/09/1918	12/09/1918
Miscellaneous	Instructions For Entrainment Etc of 21st (S) Bn. The Manchester Regt on 13th Sept 1918	12/09/1918	12/09/1918
Miscellaneous	21st (S) Bn. The Manchester Regiment.	12/09/1918	12/09/1918
Miscellaneous	21st (S) Battalion The Manchester Regiment. Appendix A		
Miscellaneous	Appendix B.		
Miscellaneous	Appendix C		
Miscellaneous	Reinforcements for the Month of September. 1918		
Miscellaneous			
Miscellaneous	Amendment to Instructions For Entrainment		
Miscellaneous	Appendix D.		
Miscellaneous	March Table To Accompany O.O. 152		
Miscellaneous	Move of Regimental Transport	25/09/1918	25/09/1918
Miscellaneous	March Table to accompany 7th Inf Bde No.SC. 21/23 of 25th September, 1918		
Miscellaneous	Captain H. Buckley, M.C.	26/09/1918	26/09/1918
Miscellaneous	Captain W.H.Cox.	26/09/1918	26/09/1918
Miscellaneous			
Miscellaneous	9th Devonshire Rgt 106 Field Coy.	26/09/1918	26/09/1918
Operation(al) Order(s)	21st (S) Battalion The Infantry Regiment O.O. 153	26/09/1918	26/09/1918
Miscellaneous	21st (S) Battalion The Worcester Regiment.		
Miscellaneous	Administrative Orders for Move By Train on 27th Sept., 1918	26/09/1918	26/09/1918
Miscellaneous	Entraining Programme		
Miscellaneous	Messages And Signals.	28/09/1918	28/09/1918
Miscellaneous	Warning Order	28/09/1918	28/09/1918
Operation(al) Order(s)	7th Infantry Brigade Order No.1	30/09/1918	30/09/1918
Operation(al) Order(s)	Operation Order No 154	29/09/1918	29/09/1918
War Diary	Lieramont Area	01/10/1918	01/10/1918
War Diary	Ronssoy Area	02/10/1918	02/10/1918
War Diary	In the Line	03/10/1918	11/10/1918
War Diary	Elincourt	12/10/1918	17/10/1918
War Diary	Maurois	18/10/1918	18/10/1918
War Diary	In the line	19/10/1918	29/10/1918
War Diary	Pommereuil Le Cateau	30/10/1918	31/10/1918
War Diary		03/10/1918	11/10/1918
Miscellaneous	Special Order	16/10/1918	16/10/1918

Type	Title	Date From	Date To
Miscellaneous	Special Order	17/10/1918	17/10/1918
War Diary		19/10/1918	24/10/1918
Miscellaneous	Reinforcement For The March At October 1918		
Miscellaneous	75th Infantry Brigade Instructions No. 1 Series "A"	31/10/1918	31/10/1918
War Diary	Le Cateau	01/11/1918	02/11/1918
War Diary	In the Line	03/11/1918	07/11/1918
War Diary	Dompierre Mariolles	08/11/1918	09/11/1918
War Diary	Landrecies	10/11/1918	12/11/1918
War Diary	Pommereuil	13/11/1918	27/11/1918
War Diary	Posemutl	28/11/1918	29/11/1918
War Diary	Quievy	30/11/1918	30/11/1918
Miscellaneous	Month Of November 1918	02/12/1918	02/12/1918
Miscellaneous	App 3	02/11/1918	02/11/1918
Miscellaneous	75th Infantry Brigade Instructions No 2-Series "A"	02/11/1918	02/11/1918
Miscellaneous	7th Infantry Brigade Instructions No 1	02/11/1918	02/11/1918
Miscellaneous	Owen to Bade		
Miscellaneous	Instructions in Connection With Move of the Battalion to-Day	03/11/1918	03/11/1918
Miscellaneous	7th Infantry Brigade Instructions No 2		
Miscellaneous	7th Infantry Brigade Instructions No 6	03/11/1918	03/11/1918
Miscellaneous	7th Infantry Brigade Instructions No. 3	03/11/1918	03/11/1918
Miscellaneous	75th Infantry Brigade Instructions No. 4 Series "A"	03/11/1918	03/11/1918
Miscellaneous	App-I	10/11/1918	10/11/1918
Miscellaneous	Casualties for the Month of November. 1918		
War Diary		03/11/1918	08/11/1918
Operation(al) Order(s)	7th Infantry Brigade Order No. 24	05/11/1918	05/11/1918
Miscellaneous	Special Order	11/11/1918	11/11/1918
Operation(al) Order(s)	21st Bn. The Manchester Regiment. Operation Order No. 161	13/11/1918	13/11/1918
Operation(al) Order(s)	21st Bn. The Manchester Regiment Operation Order No. 162	28/11/1918	28/11/1918
Operation(al) Order(s)	7th Infantry Brigade Order No. 27	28/11/1918	28/11/1918
Miscellaneous	March Table		
Miscellaneous	War Diary for Month of December 1918	01/01/1918	01/01/1918
War Diary	Quievy	01/12/1918	27/12/1918
War Diary	Bethencourt	28/12/1918	31/12/1918
Miscellaneous	Reinforcements for the Month of December 1918		
Miscellaneous	7th Infantry Brigade No. S.764/400/19 App 1	24/12/1918	24/12/1918
Operation(al) Order(s)	21st Bn. The Manchester Regiment. Operation Order No. 163	27/12/1918	27/12/1918
Miscellaneous	21st (S) Battalion The Manchester Regiment. App 2.	26/12/1918	26/12/1918
Miscellaneous	War Diary for Month of January 1919	02/02/1919	02/02/1919
War Diary	Bethencourt	01/01/1919	02/01/1919
War Diary	Poix Du Nord	03/01/1919	31/01/1919
Miscellaneous	21st bn. The Manchester Regiment. Warning Order No. 2	01/01/1919	01/01/1919
Miscellaneous	21st Bn. The Manchester Regiment. Warning Order	01/01/1919	01/01/1919
Operation(al) Order(s)	21st Bn. The Manchester Regiment. Operation Order No. 164	02/01/1919	02/01/1919
Miscellaneous	Reinforcements for The Month Of January 1919		
Miscellaneous	War Diary For Month Of January. 1919	02/03/1919	02/03/1919
War Diary	Poix Du Nord	01/02/1919	19/02/1919
War Diary	Solesmes	20/02/1919	20/02/1919
War Diary	Cambrai	21/02/1919	28/02/1919
Miscellaneous	Reinforcements for the month of February 1919		
Miscellaneous	7th Infantry Brigade No. B.M. 431	15/02/1919	15/02/1919

Miscellaneous	7th Infantry Brigade No. B.M. 434	16/02/1919	19/02/1919
Operation(al) Order(s)	7th Infantry Brigade Order No. 31	16/02/1919	16/02/1919
Miscellaneous	March Table		
Miscellaneous	Administrative Instructions In Connection With 7th Brigade Order No. 31	17/02/1919	17/02/1919
Miscellaneous			
Miscellaneous	Administrative Instructions To Accompany O.O. No. 165		
Operation(al) Order(s)	21st Battalion The Manchester Regiment. Operation Order No 165		
War Diary	Oambrai	01/03/1919	31/03/1919
Miscellaneous	List of Casualties for the Month of March	17/03/1919	17/03/1919
War Diary	Cambrai	01/04/1919	30/04/1919
Miscellaneous	Reinforcements for the Month of April. 1919	15/04/1919	15/04/1919
War Diary	Cambrai	01/05/1919	30/06/1919
War Diary	Cambrai	01/07/1919	04/07/1919
War Diary	On the Move	05/07/1919	05/07/1919

No. 05/22441 S

XXV

7 Bde M Gun Coy

Feb.

Vol 2

25TH DIVISION
7TH INFY BDE

21ST BN MANCHESTER REGT
SEP 1918-JLY 1919

From Italy 7 Div. 91 Bde

Army Form C. 2118.

WAR DIARY
or
INTELLIGENCE SUMMARY.

Volume 35.
September 1918.

21st (S) Battalion The Manchester Regiment.

Place	Date	Hour	Summary of Events and Information	Remarks and references to Appendices.
ARZIGNANO.	1		In Billets Training Fine.	
do	2		do do Wet.	
do	3		do The Battalion attended Divisional Sports at TRISSINO. Fine.	
do	4		do Training. Fine.	
do	5		do Outpost Scheme carried out at Night. Fine.	
do	6		do Fine.	
do	7		do Route March&Battle Order(from 6.30 am. to 10.30 am) Fine.	
do	8		do Stormy.	
do	9		do Training Fine.	
do	10		do do do	
do	11		do do do	
do	12		do do Fine.	
do	13		do Inspection by G.O.C. 7th Division. Fine.	
On the Train.			The Bn. left ARZIGNANO for France. "C" "D" half "H.Q. Coys and half Regt. Transport left at 1 pm. "Remaining half Bn. at 5 pm. Entrainment took place at TAVERNELLE, first half Bn. leaving at 5.11 pm. second half at 10.11 pm.	
do	14		First Train arrived MILANO 8.30 am.TORINO 4 pm. MODANE 10 pm. Fine.	
			Second do do do 10.00 am. do 7 pm. do 11.45 pm.	
			At Midnight Bn. came on the strength of 25th Division.	
do	15		First Train DIJON at noon. Second a few minutes later. do	
do	16		Environs of PARIS about 9 a.m.- Both Trains. AMIENS 3.45 pm.ABBEVILLE 7 pm. St.RIQUIER 8 pm. at St.RIQUIER Bn. detrained 1st train being immediately by second. Half Battalions marched independently to NEUILLY- l'hopital. All in Billets by 11 pm. Fine.	
NEUILLY- l'hopital.	17		In billets. Training Fine.	
do	18		do do do	
do	19		do do do	
do	20		do Practice Outpost Scheme. Showery.	
do	21		do Training. Lectures by Divnl.Gas Officer. Showery.	
do	22		do Fine.	
do	23		do Training do	
do	24		do Tactical Exercises. Fair.	
do	25		do Training Showery.	

WAR DIARY
INTELLIGENCE SUMMARY

Army Form C. 2118.

Volume 35.
September 1918.

Place	Date	Hour	Summary of Events and Information	Remarks and references to Appendices
NEUILLY L'Hôpital	26		Support Scheme carried out. 1st/4th Bn/Y's Transport moved to ST SAVEUR and stayed the night.	A
Fm. du Gard	27		Bn. left NEUILLY at 2.30 pm - marched to ST SAVEUR - entrained 5.44 pm. Proceeding by Troop train to arr 10.20 pm - marched to PONTE-REMY - arrived 7.35 pm. Bn. Transport arr at ST SAVEUR - moved to FRANVILLERS	A 449, 72, 7A A
FRANVILLERS	28		Bn. bivouac ALBERT about 1 am - marched to FRANVILLERS - arr Bn. at FRANVILLERS 12.30 pm. Bn. Transport 9 Cooker and grms. Bn. on arr FRANVILLERS began...	A
PONT NOYELLES(? near Albert)	29		Transport left Fm MONTAUBAN at 8 am. Bn. left by Motor Lorry at 10.30 am - arr in MONTAUBAN 3.30 pm. Bn arr in bivouacs at Fm. near 12.30 pm. Training.	A
	30		List of reinforcements and casualties attached.	A

[signature]
Lt Col.
Commdg 1/4th Battalion The Hampshire Regiment

SECRET/   21st (S) Battalion The MANCHESTER Regiment.   Copy No......

OPERATION ORDER NO. 152.

REF Map.- THA BRENTA di PIAVE 1/100,000.   12th SEPTEMBER, 1918.

1. The 21st Bn. The MANCHESTER Regiment is to be transferred from the 91st Infantry Brigade to another Infantry Brigade in FRANCE.

2. The Battalion will entrain at TAVERNELLE in two trains:-

   First Train dep: 5.11 p.m. 13th inst.-conveying C & D. Coys.) :-
   Second do. dep:10.30 p.m. 13th inst.-   "   A & B. Coys.)

   and a proportion of Bn.H.Q. and Transport as laid down in Appendices A & B. attached to Instructions for Entrainment.

3. Troops will be at entraining station one hour and transport three hours before the advertised time of departure of the trains.
   Loading party is being provided by 20th Infantry Brigade.

4. MARCH TABLE for march to TAVERNELLE is attached.

5. ACKNOWLEDGE.

                                        E.+ Orsill
                                              Captain & Adjt,
Issued at 10/pm BY RUNNER. 21st (S) Bn. The Manchester Regiment.

DISTRIBUTION.

   1. Commanding Officer.   10. O.C. D. Company.
   2. Second In Command.   11. Transport Officer.
   3. Adjutant.   12. Ass.T.O.
   4. Assistant Adjutant.   13. Q.M.
   5. H.Q.Coy. (2 copies).   14. R.Q.M.S.
                                        15. R.S.M.
   7. O.C. A. Company.   16. 91st Infantry Brigade.
   8. O.C. B.   do.   17. File. (2 copies).
   9. O.C. C.   do.   19. WAR DIARY (2 copies).

SECRET / "INSTRUCTIONS FOR ENTRAINMENT ETC"
of 21st (S) Bn. The MANCHESTER Regt. on 12th Sept. 1918.

12th September, 1918.

1. ACCOMMODATION.

   Two trains, composed of two 1st Class Coaches - 25 Covered Vans - 11 Flats and 2 Brake Vans each are allotted to the Battalion:-

   Half Bn.H.Q. C & D. Coys will travel in First Train.
   Half Bn.H.Q. A & B. Coys. will travel in Second Train.

   A proportion of Regimental Transport will travel in each train. Appendices marked A & B. showing distribution of H.Q.Coy. and Transport are attached (for those concerned only).

2. OFFICERS.
   The Commanding Officer, Adjutant, Quartermaster and Acting Transport Officer will travel in the First Train.
   The Second In Command, Assistant Adjutant, Transport Officer and Medical Officer will travel in Second Train.

3. RATIONS.
   (a) Rations for consumption on the 13th will be issued on 12th and carried on the man.
   (b) 7 days rations on scale laid down in Appendix "C" will be carried in Q.M.Store Trucks.
   (c) The Supply (A.S.C.) Waggons will be entrained loaded with one days Preserved Rations for use on the day following day of detrainment.
   (d) It is possible that bread will be issued at ST. GERMAIN MONT D'OR.

4. HALTES REPAS.
   (a) A time table and list of Haltes Repas will be issued as soon as possible.
   (b) A horse ramp will be available at each Haltes Repas.

5. BAGGAGE.
   (a) Officers Valises and mess kit they require on the journey will be loaded and carried in Officers Compartments.
   (b) A.S.C. Train Waggons will be loaded and distributed on trains as follows:-

   Each Train (1 waggon. (half load of supplies.
              ((half load of forage.
              (1 waggon. (half load of Q.M.Stores.
              ((half load of Officers valises.

   (Officers valises to be unloaded at entraining station and reloaded at detraining station (see (a) above).

   (c) On arrival at entraining station troops will pick up their packs and steel helmets before entraining. After entrainment has been completed 1 man per section will be marched by Company Orderly Sergeants to the blanket dump where they will collect the blankets belonging to their respective section and load them in the trucks occupied by their sections. N.C.Os. i/c of workshops etc. will be entirely responsible that if their kits have not been loaded before they themselves arrive, this is done before the train departs.

6. **TRANSPORT.**
See Appendix G.O. (issued to Transport Officer only).

7. **ENTRAINMENT.**
Seconds In Command of Companies will meet the Adjutants of their particular train one hour before their half battalion is due to entrain.
Accomodation for their Companies will be allotted to them and any further instructions that are necessary issued verbally to them.

8. **DUTIES ON THE TRAIN.**
   (a) An Orderly Officer will be detailed daily by the O.C. Train. His tour of duty will be from 12 midnight - 12 midnight. He will be the last officer to entrain and will ensure and report to the Adjutant that all ranks are on board 5 minutes prior to the departure of the train. His duties on the train will be:-
   1. To see that guards are properly mounted at each recognised halt.
   2. To see that no man leaves the train when it halts unless authorised to do so.
   3. To ensure that no men ride onx the steps or climb along the train from truck to truck.
   4. Fall in the Orderlymen of Companies and Headquarters and march them to the Stores van for rations.
   5. Report to the Adjutant when meals are ready.
   (b) **DUTIES OF GUARDS.**
   1. See paras (b) and (c) above.
   2. Companies will provide guards of 1 N.C.O. & 6 O.Rs. for their respective ends of the train.
   (c) **DUTIES OF COMPANY ORDERLY SERGEANTS.**
   To parade Orderlymen with dixies at recognised halts opposite their Company carriage or van, and then proceed under the Orderly Officer as in para (d) above.
   1. To ensure that no other men leave the train without orders.
   2. To ensure that where no latrines exist sanitarymen dig them and fill them in prior to departure of train.
   3. To report any damage done to waggons to the Adjutant of the train.

9. **BUGLE CALLS.**
The "DISMISS" will be sounded as a signal that personnel may leave the train.
On the "FALLIN" being sounded all ranks will immediately return to their trucks.
Any other calls sounded will be promptly obeyed.

10. **MEDICAL.**
A truck will be set aside on each train for an AID POST. Sick Parades will be held immediately on arrival at a Halte Repas. O.C. Companies will ensure that Company Sanitarymen are in possession of 2 shovels and 2 brooms, if possible. Shovels may be drawn from Transport Officer.

11. **DETRAINMENT.**
On arrival at detraining station:-
   (a) On 1st G. sounding Platoon Sergeants will detrain and stand clear of and facing away from the train.
   (b) On the 2nd G. sounding men will detrain and fall in on their Platoon Sergeants in silence.
   (c) Officers will supervise the detraining of their Companies and platoons.
   (d) All loading and unloading duties will be carried out by parties detailed by R.T.O. at entraining and detraining stations respectively.

- 3 -

12. ACKNOWLEDGE.

                                        Captain & Adjutant,
                              21st (S) Bn. The Manchester Regiment.
Issued at   BY RUNNER.

DISTRIBUTION.

To all recipients of O.O.152.

SECRET/ 21st (S) Bn. The MANCHESTER Regiment.   Copy No....

ADMINISTRATIVE INSTRUCTIONS for
Move to Entraining Station Sep.15th,1918.

12th SEPTEMBER, 1918.

1. DRESS.- Battle Order.

2. LORRIES.- Four 3 ton lorries will report to Quartermaster at 10 a.m. 15th instant and are available all day.

3. BAGGAGE.
All blankets, packs with steel helmets strapped to them, workshops kit, cooks kit, officers valises, officers mess kit, Orderly Room kit and Aid Post Kit will be stacked at Q.M.Stores at 10.0 a.m. for those detailed for 1st train and at 3.30 p.m. for those detailed for 2nd train.
In the case of workshops etc. whose personnel are divided between the two trains - steps will be taken to ensure their baggage is also evenly divided and loaded at the right time.

4. Loading Parties.
O.C. C & D. & 1st Half H.Q.Coy. will detail 1 man per section to report at Quartermaster's Stores at 10 a.m. in full marching order.
O.C. A & B. & 2nd Half H.Q.Coy. will detail 1 man per section to report at Quartermaster's Stores at 3.30 p.m. in full marching order.

Issued at 8/h BY RUNNER.

H. Orgill
Captain & Adjutant,
21st Bn. The MANCHESTER Regiment.

DISTRIBUTION.

To all recipients of O.O.182.

21st (S) Battalion The LANCASTER Regiment.

APPENDIX A.

Distribution of Headquarter Company.

1st TRAIN.		2nd TRAIN.
2	H.Q. & Batmen.	nil
nil.	C.S.M. & Coy. Clerk.	2
23	Signallers.	nil.
nil.	Band.	nil.
	Buglers.	
nil.	Snipers.	
3	Scouts.	3
	Bn. Orderly Room.	nil.
5	Rum Rs.	5
3	Q.M. Stores.	3
6	Servants.	3
1	M.O. Orderlies.	1
	Cooks.	
	Pioneers.	
1	Contnn.	
2	Shoemakers.	2
1	Tailor.	
nil.	Instructional Staff.	
nil.	Countrymen	
2	Prisoners.	1
71	TOTAL.	**69**

APPENDIX B.

	1st Train								2nd Train					
	Pack	Riders	T.D.	W.D.	Extra	Vehicles	O.R.	Off.	O.R.	Vehicles	Extra	W.D.	T.D.	Riders	Pack
Personnel.							28	1	23						
Cookers.				2	2	1				2					
G.S. Wagon.			1	2	4	1				2	4		1		
L.G. Limbers.			2		2	1				1	2		2		
S.A.A. Limbers.			2		5	1				1	5		2		
Tool Limber.			1		2	1				1	2		1		
Water Cart.			1			1				1	1		1		
Grenade Limber.															
Maltese Cart.					1	1						1			
Hose Cart.															
Chargers.				2											
Pack.	4													5	5
Spare		5													
TOTAL.	4	5	13	4	14	6	28	1	23	10	19	5	15	5	5

APPENDIX C.

8 days rations for following scale are
loaded on train.

Condensed Milk.	1 oz.
Preserved Meat.	9 ozs.
Bread. (for 2 days only).	16 ozs.
Biscuit (for 6 days only).	12 ozs.
Sugar.	3 ozs. or when sweetened condensed milk is issued one & half ozs.
Jam.	3 ozs.
Cheese.	3 ozs.
Tea.	half oz.
Rum	1/64th gall.) one issue for one
Matches.	1 box.)
Tobacco or Cigarettes	2 ozs.) day only.
Solidified Paraffin.	2 ozs.)
Forage in accordance with G.R.O. ITALY nO;674.	
FUEL.	8 days fuel for cookers.

Reinforcements for the Month of September, 1918.

Date	Officers	Other Ranks
27/8/18.		1 Other Rank.
31/8/18.		14 do
4/9/18.		12 do
7/9/18.		1 do
8/9/18.		1 do
9/9/18.		1 do
10/9/18.		1 do
13/9/18.		4 do
25/9/18.		1 do
23/9/18.	1 Officer.	
26/9/18.		2 do

Casualties for the Month of September, 1918.

NIL.

Staff Captain,
17th Brigade,

Could you please arrange for Private Losey to report here in order that I may return Salvage and soiled Underclothing to ST. RIQUIER, as I have not transport available.

Chittaway Lieut. Colonel
Commdg. 21st Manchester Regiment
25/9/1918

O.C. 21 Manchester Regt.

See my E/11 re removal of Salvage.

Dirty underclothing which is in a serviceable condition must be sent to O.C. Divisional Laundry, at ST. RIQUIER.

N.F. White

SECRET/ AMENDMENT to "INSTRUCTIONS FOR EMBARKMENT"

Delete para. 3 (b) and substitute:-

"3 (b) A supply and a baggage waggons will be at the disposal of Quartermaster for one journey each to entraining station - they will not accompany the Battalion to FRANCE."

                                           Captain & Adjt.
                                    21st (S) Bn. Manchester Regiment.

DISTRIBUTION.
To all recipients of C.O.152.

APPENDIX D.

HORSES.

(a) Whenever possible, accomodation for saddlery and gear should be found in trucks, other than those used by the horses.
(b) Not more than 8 R.D. Horses should be put in one truck. Higher trucks should be reserved for H.D.Horses.
(c) No Oats will be fed for the first 12 hours after entraining.
(d) Hay nets and water buckets will be taken up to the full scale allowed.
(e) Tails will be bandaged whenever possible before entrainment, and care will be taken that horses are not tied too far back in the trucks.
(f) If possible ashes or sand should be placed in the trucks to give foot-hold. This must be arranged by Units at the entraining station.
(g) Units to be complete with one horse-rug, but these rugs only to be used on clipped horses.
(h) Ventilation of trucks is most important and should be regulated according to whether the truck is in motion or halted.
Pneumonia was caused on the move from France to Italy in several cases by insufficient ventilation having been given during the journey.
(i) The door on the side of the running way must be kept closed.
(j) Personnel of A.V.C. should be distributed between trains to the best advantage.
(k) Galvanised pails, petrol tins or paraffin tins, up to a capacity of 24 gallons per truck, will be supplied for carrying water. These will be provided at entraining railheads under Divisional arrangements.
(l) Water will be available at each Halte Repas.
(m) Cooking and fires of any description are forbidden in horse trucks.
(n) Horses will be entrained by their own drivers, and not by the fatigue party.
(o) Great care must be taken to see that horses are securely roped in the trucks, as during previous movements of troops, accidents occurred owing to lack of this precaution.
All the ropes are to be provided by the Unit.

1/... the WORCESTER Regiment.

MARCH TABLE to accompany O.O.152.

UNIT (in order of march)	Starting Pt.	Time.	ROUTE.	Time of departure of Train from TAVERNELLE.
1st Half Regt. Transport. 1st Half Bn. H.Q. Coy. C. Company. D. Company.	Bn. H.Q.	11. 0 a.m. 1 p.m. 5.30 p.m.	ARZIGNANO - Id. Junction immediately N. of I. of VIGALE - MONTECCHIO MAGGIORE - TAVERNELLE.	5.11 p.m.
2nd Half Regt. Transport. 2nd Half Bn. H.Q. Coy. Band. A. Company. B. Company.	A. Company's billet.	6.30 p.m.		10.30 p.m.

A 21/23

SECRET

MOVE of REGIMENTAL TRANSPORT.

Re 1/100,000 ABBEVILLE, LENS and AMIENS Sheets.

1. All transport of following units, except wagons, etc., stated in para. 2, will march to-day.

2. The following will <u>not</u> march but will entrain with units on 27th.

      Brigade H.Q. ... 1 Baggage wagon: 4 Riding Horses
      Each Infantry Battn ... 1 Lewis Gun limbered wagon.
            3 Cookers, 1 Cooks' wagon.
            2 Water carts
            1 Mess Cart.
            2 Baggage wagons.
            5 Riding horses.

      106th Field Coy, R.E.   1 Wagon
                               1 Water Cart

      201st Coy A.S.C.   1 G.S. Wagon.

3. Lt.-Col. F.L. LORD, D.S.O., A.S.C., will be in command of troops and transport on the march.
O.C., 201st Coy A.S.C. will be in charge of transport of this Brigade Group.

4. The march will be continued on 26th and 27th inst. to Fourth Army area.

5. Rations for consumption 26th and 27th will be carried

Rations for consumption 28th will be drawn on morning of 27th from A.S.C., AILLY SUR SOMME.

6. Fifty-five boxes of S.A.A. will be withdrawn from Units to-day, to enable them to carry on the limbered G.S. wagon thus emptied, additional Lewis Guns and magazines now held on charge.

7. Further instructions re disposal of Practice ammunition and salvage will be issued.

88. <u>ACKNOWLEDGE.</u>

Captain.
Staff Captain, 7th Inf. Bde

25 September, 1918

Issued at 11.0 am.

Copies to :-

1. 9th Devonshire Regt   201st Coy A.S.C
2. 20th Manchester Regt   Brigade Sergt
   21st Manchester Regt
   106th Field Coy, R.E.

MARCH TABLE to accompany 7th Inf.Bde No.3O G/25
of 25th September, 1918

Transport of Unit	From	To	Starting Point	Time	Route
201st Coy A.S.C.	NEUF MOULIN / DRUCAT	FLIXECOURT - LOURDON	Level crossing one mile S.W. of ST. RIQUIER.	2.40 pm	YAUCOURT - BUSSUS - AILLY LE HAUT - CLOCHER LA FOLIE
20th Manchester Regt.	DRUCAT	do.	do.	2.45 pm	do
1Oth Field Coy, R.E.	LE PLESSIEL	do.	do.	2.45 pm	do
21st Manchester Regt	BRUILLE L'HOPITAL	do.	do.	2.45 pm	do } No details fixed via NEUILLY HOSPITAL
9th Devonshire Regt.	CANCHY	do	do.	2.45 pm	do } DRUCAT - COQUES - NEUF MOULIN
7th Infantry Brigade H.Q.	CANCHY	do	do.	2.45 pm	do

Allots will be allotted by O.C. 25th Divisional Train.

One hundred yards distance will be maintained between transport of Units.

* * * * *

Captain H. BUCKLEY, M.C.   *Secret*

> 21ST (S) BATTALION,
> THE MANCHESTER
> REGIMENT.
> No. M1662
> Date ....

Reference move of 25th Division by tactical trains to-morrow.
You have been detailed as one of the Divisional Detraining Officer at EDGEHILL.
You will proceed by the 1st train leaving PONT REMY i.e.(13.17).
You should report to the R.T.O. one hour before this time.
The transports of units detraining at EDGEHILL are detailed in the lower part of the attached time table which to-gether with the Divisional Entrainment Orders are forwarded for your information and retention.

Bn.Hd.Qtrs.
26/9/18.

Captain & Adjutant,
21st Battalion The MANCHESTER Regiment.

Secret

Captain W.H. COX.
Officer Commanding,
B. Company (for information).

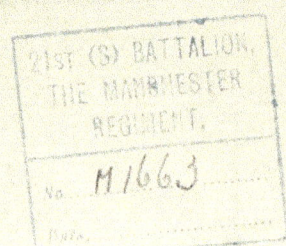

———

    Reference move of 25th Division by tactical trains to-morrow.
    You have been detailed as one of the Divisional Entraining Officers.
    You will report to the R.T.O. ST. RIQUIER one and a half hours before the departure of the 1st train i.e., at 10.10 a.m.
    You will travel by the last train leaving ST RIQUIER (18.41).
    Copy of the Divisional Entrainment Orders are attached for your information and retention.

Bn.Hd.Qtrs.
26/9/18.

Captain & Adjutant,
21st Battalion The MANCHESTER Regiment.

Q.M. 12

Head Quarters
7th Brigade

Reference your E.11.
Lorry required for two journeys, to report to these Head quarters at 2.30 p.m.

B. Ingham
Lieut-Colonel
Commdg 21st Manchester Regiment

26/9/1918

21 Manchester Regt.

You should not have more than one half a lorry load.

You have two baggage wagons for ordinary baggage and blankets are not to be sent by lorry.

This lorry can however do one journey for you but the driver has instructions to get back quickly to work for other Batteries.

H.P. White

9th Devonshire Regt   108 Field Coy,   B.11
20th Manchester Regt   R.E.
21st Manchester Regt
======================================

       Re move tomorrow.

       Division regret that they will have no lorries to spare to-morrow to convey surplus baggage to entraining station for animals and vehicles (PONT REMY).

       Troops will entrain at St. RIVIER.

       I have one lorry at the disposal of the whole Brigade to-day, in which such baggage can be sent to PONT REMY to await arrival of transport vehicles to-morrow.

       Please say <u>at once</u> if you have any stores that can be sent to-day, stating approximately the amount of room they will take up in a lorry.

       In selecting stores to be sent in this manner, the question of moving them from the detraining station will have to be considered, as there may be no lorries available at the other end.

       Target material should be taken.

       Men's blankets will either be carried on the men or on transport vehicles.

       The Divisional Salvage Officer will also endeavour to send a lorry round to-day to collect salvage.

                                      Captain,
26 Sept 1918   Staff Captain, 7th Infantry Bde

Reply:
Lorry required for our baggage...

OO.153

ORDER/ 21st (S) Battalion The Manchester Regiment. Order No. 8.

Reference Sheets:- ABBEVILLE - LENS & AMIENS
1/100,000.

26th February, 1918.

1. The 35th Division will move by tactical trains to the ALBERT Area to-morrow 27th instant.

2. The Battalion (less transport) will entrain together with Brigade H.Q. & 16th Bn. Manchester Regiment at ST. RIQUIER at **16.47**. train departs one hour later.

3. Transport will entrain at PORT REMY at 16.01 train departs three hours later.
   Detraining Stations:-
        For Battalion = ALBERT.
        For transport = ACHEUX.
   The journey will take approximately **4** hours.

4. The Battalion and transport will march out in accordance with the attached "March Table".

5. Companies and transport will render "ENTRAINING STATES" to Battalion Orderly Room by **11** a.m.

6. The entrainments must be completed half an hour before the time of the departure of the train.

7. All doors of covered trucks and carriages on the right hand side of the train when on the main line must be kept closed.

8. The transport will not enter the station yard before the R.T.O. is ready.

9. Water Carts will travel full, waterbottles will be filled and horses watered before leaving.

10. BAGGAGE ARRANGEMENTS.
    (a) COOKS baggage will be ready for loading at 12. 5 p.m.
        One G.S. waggon will report at B.H.Qrs at **12** noon, load up with H.Q. Officers valises, mess kit, Orderly Room Boxes and Elements of the band and then report in Transport Yard and complete its load with officers valises.
        All Company Officers valises will be ready for loading in Transport Yard at **11. 30** a.m.
        Mess Cart will report to B. Coy. Officers Mess at **11. 40** a.m. and then tow A. & C. Coys.

    (b) One Officers servant per Company, 1 cook per Company and one Orderly Room Clerk will report to the transport Officer in the Transport Yard at **12. 20** p.m. They will march out entrain with the transport. On no account will anyone else be permitted to march with the transport.

11. ACKNOWLEDGE.

T Y Gill

Issued at 2 a.m. 27/2/1 Captain,
                        for Adjt., 21st Bn. Manchester Regiment.

DISTRIBUTION.
1. Commanding Officer.
2 - 6. O.C. All Coys.
7. Capt. & T.O.
8. File.
9 - 10. War Diary.

21st (S) Battalion The WESTERN Regiment.

MARCH TABLE to accompany O.O.18.

UNIT in order of march.	Starting pt.	Time.	ROUTE.	Entraining station and time of departure of train.	Detraining station.
Band. B. Coy. A. " D. " C. " H.Q. "	300 yds. E. of Church on ST. NICHOLAS Rd.	2.45 p.m.	Direct. (6 km.)	ST. NICHOLAS. 5.47 p.m.	ALBERT.
TRANSPORT personnel detailed in para. 10 (b) of O.O. 18.	Bn. H.Q.	12.21 p.m.	INJERT GAOUR VACQUELESS- lez-DEBEY N'ADAM MEULINE- sur-SOHN FORT EELY (15 km.)	FORT EELY. 7.21 p.m.	MORAIL (about one - half mile S. of ALBERT.)

MESS for all.- Full marching order. Blanket strapped on top of pack - steel helmets will be worn.

ADMINISTRATIVE ORDERS for MOVE BY TRAIN
on 27th Sept., 1918.
****

SC 21/24

1. (a) The Division, less Artillery, Pioneer and M.G. Battalions, and less units and transport that proceeded by march route on 25th inst., will entrain to-morrow, 27th inst., in accordance with attached table.

2. Troops will entrain at St. RIQUIER - All transport and horses at PONT REMY. Six tactical trains will be provided for troops - Three trains for transport. The journey is expected to take about four hours.

3. ENTRAINMENT.

   (a) The D.A.Q.M.G. will superintend the entrainment.
       His address will be c/o R.T.O., St. RIQUIER.

   (b) Entraining Officers will be detailed by units as follows:-

       At St. RIQUIER :   1 Major or Captain, 20th Manchester Rgt
                           1   "   "   "   21st   "   "

       They will report to R.T.O. St. RIQUIER one and a half hours before the departure of the first train, and will travel by the last train.

   (c) Billetting parties, as under, with bicycles, will report to the Staff Captain at St. RIQUIER Station at 10.30 a.m.

           Each Infantry Battn: One Officer, 2 Other Ranks.
           106th Field Coy R.E.:   One Officer, 1 Other Rank.

   (d) Tactical trains consist of 46 covered wagons and two Officers' coaches.
       Transport trains consist of 29 covered wagons, one Officers' coach, and 17 flat trucks.

   (e) No personnel or stores will be allowed in the brake vans at each end of the train, or on the roofs of the trucks.

   (f) Units will arrive at St. RIQUIER Station one hour before the departure of the train. Transport will arrive at PONT REMY three hours before the departure of the train.

   (g) An Officer will be detailed to command the Transport of each Infantry Battalion, and O.C. 9th Devonshire Rgt will also detail a Major to be in charge of the Transport Train leaving PONT REMY at 19.31 hours.

(1).

(h). A complete marching-out state showing the number of men, horses, G.S., Limbered G.S. and two-wheeled wagons and cycles should be sent down with each unit and with transport of each unit, so that accommodation on the train can be checked by the R.T.O. at the beginning of the entrainment, limbered G.S. wagons being counted as 2 two-wheeled vehicles on the state.

(i). The entrainment of all units must be completed half an hour before the time of departure of the train when it will be moved from the loading station.

(j). Breast ropes for horse trucks must be provided by the units themselves; ropes for lashing vehicles on the flat trucks will be provided by the railway.

(k). The O.C. each train will detail picquets for duty at all stops, to prevent troops straggling away from the train.

(l). All doors of covered trucks and carriages on the right hand side of the train, when on the main line, should be kept closed.

(m). No troops or transport will enter the station yard before the R.T.O. is ready.

4. DETRAINMENT.

(a). The D.A.A.G. will superintend the detrainment.

(b). Detraining Officers will be detailed by units as follows:-

TO GO FROM PONT REMY :- 1 Major or Captain, 20th Manchester Rgt
                         1   "   "   "   21st Manchester Rgt

Capt Buckley

They will proceed by first train from PONT REMY, and report to R.T.O. at the detraining Station.
They will be provided with a list of Units arriving at their detraining Station, and will receive details as regards billetting, etc., from the D.A.A.G.

(c). O.C. 9th Devonshire Rgt will detail a party of one Officer and 50 other ranks for duty unloading at the detraining station. This party will proceed by the first train from PONT REMY, and will report to R.T.O. at detraining station.

(d) Detraining stations are:-

ALBERT for troops.   EDGEHILL for transport.

5. SUPPLIES.

Rations for 27th will be carried on the men, and for animals with transport. Rations for 28th will be delivered to Units on arrival in new billets.

6. Water carts will travel full.   Waterbottles will be filled and

horses watered before leaving.

                                                                       Captain,

26 Sept., 1918.   Staff Captain, 7th Inf.Bde

Issued to :-

       1. 9th Devonshire Rgt
       2. 20th Manchester Rgt
       3. 21st Manchester Rgt
       4. 106th Field Company, R.E.
       5. G. O. C.
       6. Brigade Major
       7. Staff Captain

                              * * * * *

ENTRAINING PROGRAMME.

Entraining Station :-   Detraining Station :-
ST. RIQUIER.   ALBERT.

PERSONNEL.

Train No.	UNIT.	Date.	Time of Departure.
1.	x x x x x x x 201st Company, A.S.C.	27th	11.40
7.	H.Q., 7th Inf. Bde) 20th Manchester Rgt) 21st Manchester Rgt)	"	17.47
8.	9th Devonshire Rgt) 106th Field Coy, R.E.)	"	18.41

TRANSPORT.

Entraining Station :-   Detraining Station :-
PONT REMY.   EDGEHILL.

Train No.	UNIT.	Date	Time of Departure.
9.	H.Q., 7th Inf. Bde) 9th Devonshire Rgt) 20th Manchester Rgt) 21st Manchester Rgt) 106th Field Coy, R.E.) 201st Company, A.S.C.)	27th	19.31

MESSAGES AND SIGNALS.

Army Form C. 2121.
(In pads of 100.)

TO
9 Devons.   108 Fd Co R.E.
11 Man.   201 Co RSC
11 Man.   77 F.A.

Sender's Number: W 33
Day of Month: 28
AAA

Re move tomorrow to GUILLEMONT Area aaa
Billetting parties will meet the Staff Captain at Area Commandants office MONTAUBAN at 10.30 am

It is hoped to send lorries ~~temporarily~~ (at the rate of one half lorry per unit as above) to pick up surplus baggage aaa

Such should be left in charge of a man on the lookout for the lorry

From: 7 Bde

S E C R E T.

W A R N I N G   O R D E R.

    Division will be prepared to move to CARNOY Area by bus about mid-day tomorrow 29th inst.

    Transport will move by road about 8.0 a.m. same day.

[signature]

Captain.
Brigade Major, 7th Infantry Brigade.

28/9/18.

Copies to :-

    9th Devon Regt.
    20th Manchester Regt.
    21st Manchester Regt.
    106th Field Coy. R.E.
    201st Coy. A.S.C.

SECRET.   Copy No. 3

7th INFANTRY BRIGADE ORDER NO.1.

Reference. LENS 11 and ALBERT 17.
1/100,000.

1.   7th Infantry Brigade Group will move to the GUILLEMONT Area tomorrow 29th September 1918.

2.   Transport of all Units of the Group will move by road in accordance with attached March Table.

3.   Personnel will be conveyed by motor bus from cross roads ½ mile SOUTH EAST of FRANVILLERS CHURCH, onbussing to commence at 11.30 a.m.
        Detail Orders for the embussing will be forwarded early tomorrow morning 29th inst.

4.   Orders for billetting parties and lorry detail will be forwarded later.

5.   Watches will be synchronized before 10.0 a.m. 29th inst. under arrangements to be made by Brigade Signal Officer.

6.   ACKNOWLEDGE.

                                            R.M. Burn
                                                    Captain.
                                    Brigade Major, 7th Infantry Brigade.

28/9/18.

Issued at 11 p.m.

Copies to:-
1. 9th Devon Regt.
2. 20th Manchester Regt.
3. 21st Manchester Regt.
4. 77th Field Ambulance.
5. 106th Field Coy. R.E.
6. 201 Coy. A.S.C.
7. Staff Captain.
8. Signal Officer.
9. Capt. R.C. Brown. (A.S.C.)
10. File.
11. War Diary.
12. 25th Division

Operation Order No. 139
R/ Sens-Amiens /roads   29/9/18

1/ The Bn will be moved to [?] Cernennes
   Area tomorrow
   Rest about 11am at a point ½ mile S.E.
   of Framilles Church. Full details will
   be issued later.

2/ Transport will move by road in accordance
   with march Table issued to TO. [?] bn
   will close Transport Lines 4.0am

3/ Officers Valises, Surplus kit, Surplus Cookers
   kit & Bn. kit etc. will be ready
   for loading at Bn HQ at 5.0 am.
   The following kit will be returned and checked
   by [?] to embussing point by 10.15 am
   (a) The number of drivers [?] for the Bn.
   (b) One small officers mess box /off [?]

4/ Dress full marching order, blanket rolled
   on pack, [?]

5/ Acknowledge

                              3 YC, II Bn
                         Adjt 2nd Lieut R/

Army Form C. 2118.

WAR DIARY
INTELLIGENCE SUMMARY

Volume 36.

2lst (S) Battalion heading Manchester Regiment. OCTOBER, 1918.

Place	Date	Hour	Summary of Events and Information	Remarks and references to Appendices
LIBERMONT AREA	1st		Battalion left MONTAUBAN 08.45 hrs. and marched to LIBERMONT AREA. All in bivouacs by 20.00 hrs. Continental Time (24 hrs) came into operation. Fine.	
RONSSOY Area	2nd		Training - Battalion left for RONSSOY area 16.00 hrs. In shelters by 23.00 hrs. - Fine.	
In the Line	3rd		Battalion moved to BELLICOURT in the afternoon where preparations were made for taking over the line. About 20.00 hrs. B Battalion (less B. Echelon Details and 1st Line Transport) moved forward in relief of 3 Coys. 27th Australian Infantry Battalion and 1 Company 25th Australian Infantry Battalion in the BEAUREVOIR Sector. - Fine.	
"	4th		Brigade in attack - Battalion in Reserve. - Fine.	
"	5th		Battalion in attack on PONCHAUX GENEVE & BEAUREVOIR. - Fair.	
"	6th		Battalion relieved by 9th Devons Regt. withdrew to reserve positions. - Fair.	
"	7th		Day spent in preparation for advance.	
"	8th		Battalion advanced - Reached vicinity of SERAIN. B. Echelon moved to BEAUREVOIR. - Fair.	
"	9th		In attack - At 22.00 hrs. Battalion withdrew to TROUAUX SOLDATS. B. Echelon to PREMONT - Fair.	
"	10th		In Brigade Reserve. Battalion advancing - B. Echelon at 14.00 hrs. arrived MARETZ - 18.00 hrs left for ESCAUFOURT. - Showery.	
"	11th		Resting during day - In the evening withdrew to ELINCOURT. In billets 23.02 hrs. - Fine.	
ELINCOURT	12th		In Billets. - Training. - Fair.	
"	13th		do. do. do.	
"	14th		do. do. do.	
"	15th		do. do. Snowery.	
"	16th		do. do. do.	
"	17th		do. do. Wet.	
MAUROIS.	18th		Battalion left ELINCOURT 10.20 hrs. for MAUROIS - In billets 18.30 hrs. Fine.	
In the line.	19th		Battalion relieved 1/5th Gloucester Regiment in the BASUEL Sector. front line. Battalion Headquarters at Q. 11. d. 8. 4. - Wet.	
"	20th		Local action took place in Battalion Sector. 50 prisoners and 5 machine guns being taken. Posts established on N. side of RICHMONT RIVER.- Fair.	
"	21st		Situation normal. - Day spent in preparing for an attack. - Fine.	

Army Form C. 2118.

WAR DIARY
or
INTELLIGENCE SUMMARY.

Volume 36.

OCTOBER, 1918.

21st Battalion *(Erase heading not required)* MANCHESTER Regiment.

Place	Date	Hour	Summary of Events and Information	Remarks and references to Appendices
In the line.	22nd		Preparation continued - Advanced posts withdrawn. - Fine.	app Ku
"	23rd		Day of attack (detail of which will be found in NARRATIVE attached) +Fine.	
"	24th		Battalion withdrew to POMMEREUIL 09.40 hrs. No. 2. Company attached to 20th Manchester Regiment 17.00 hrs. No. 1 Coy. and Bn.H.Q. moved into Brigade Reserve - Fine.	
"	25th		Situation Normal - Fine.	
"	26th		Battalion relieved 20th Manchester Regiment. Bn. H.Q. G. 7. a. 45. 95. 16.17 hrs. - Fine.	
"	27th		Situation Normal. - Showery.	
"	28th		do. - Fine.	
"	29th		do. do.	
POMMEREUIL	30th		Battalion withdrew to POMMEREUIL - In Billets. - Fine.	
LE CATEAU	31st		Battalion left POMMEREUIL 10.30 hrs. for LE CATEAU. - Showery. List of casualties and reinforcements attached.	

Crudance Lieutenant Colonel,
Commanding 21st. Bn. The Manchester Regiment.

21st (S) Battalion The Manchester Regiment.   SECRET/

Narrative of Operations from October 4th - October 11th 1918.

Reference Maps.-
MONTBREHAIN Edition 1A 1/20.000.
FRANCE 57bSW1/20.000.
FRANCE 57B.SE.1/20.000.
FRANCE 57b.   1/40.000.

Date.	Hour.	Narrative.
3.10.18.		ROISSOY - Battalion moved forward via GUENNEMONT FARM and BELLICOURT. Battalion relieved 3 Companies 27th Australian Infantry Battalion and 1 Company 25th Australian Infantry Battalion in the BEAUREVOIR SECTOR.
4.10.18.		Relief complete 04.00 hrs. 4th October when Battalion was disposed as follows:- Bn.H.Q. A 24 Central. Companies in trench system S. & S.E. of LORMISSET.
4.10.18.		Brigade Orders received at 05.55 hrs. that 7th Infantry Brigade would attack and capture line B. 18. a. 15. 15. - PONCHAUX (inclusive) - B II Central - B. 4.D.0.4. - GUISANCOURT FARM (inclusive) - Battalion ordered to remain in Brigade Reserve - Zero hour - 0600 hrs.
4.10.18.	18.30 hrs.	Bn.H.Q. moved forward to B. 14. c. 3. 7.
	18.50 hrs.	Warning Order to attack on 5th October received. Battalion objectives as follows.- The line GENEVE (B. 18. a. 0. 2.) - PONCHAUX - B.II central - Track Junction B. 5. central.
5.10.18.		Battalion was disposed as follows for attack.- Bn.H.Q. R.A.P. B. 14. c. 3. 7. A. Company and D. Company formed up on line B. 17. d. 8. 9. to B. 17. a. 5. 4. with objective PONCHAUX - one platoon detailed to attack GENEVE. B. Company on line via B. 16. a. 7. 2. - B. 16. b. 3. 2. with objective BEAUREVOIR as far as main road running N.E. & S.W. through village. C. Company in Reserve at B. 14. c. 9. 1. Zero hour was 06.00 hours.
5.10.18.	06.00 hrs.	Two Companies moved forward to attack PONCHAUX and GENEVE and were very heavily caught in M.G. fire from both villages. They failed to get their objective.
5.10.18.	07.20 hrs.	The Company detailed to attack BEAUREVOIR advanced according to orders and were met by very considerable M.G.fire. All the houses on the S. side of the village appeared to hold machine gunners and the Company was also shot at from the Cemetary at B. 16. b. 80; 45. The Barrage apparently had very little effect on the garrison of the village and it has been reported that practically all the shelling was of light calibre.
5.10.18.	09.30 hrs.	Situation as follows.- Railway Line held from B. 16. a. 10. 85. to B. 16. a. 7. 7. thence to B. 16. a. 9. 3. along to TORRENS CANAL to B. 16. b. 25. 20. BN; H.Q. Quarry at B. 15. c. 3. 1. R.A.P. at MUSHROOM QUARRY.
5.10.18.		Elements of 75th Brigade attacked and captured BEAUREVOIR. Several detachments of this Battalion accompanied the attack.
6.10.18.		9th Devon Regiment took over Brigade Front Line - Battalion withdrew to Quarry at B. 15. c. 3. 1. and TORRENS CANAL about B. 21. a. & b. Relief Complete at hrs. Before relief patrols were pushed out in direction of PONCHAUX and GENEVE and found both localities occupied by the enemy.
7.10.18.	04.00 hrs.	Instructions for advance received. Day spent in preparation and in refitting.

- 2 -

Date.	Hours	Narrative.
7.10.18.	04.00 hrs.	25th Division to attack on a Battalion frontage - attack to be carried out by 7th Brigade - 9th Devons to 1st objective - 21st Manchester Regiment to 2nd objective - 20th Manchester Regiment in Reserve. Boundaries - On Right - B. 17. d. 3. 6. - Rd.Junction B. 17. d. 7. 8. - BRONX FARM (exclusive) to SONIA WOOD (inclusive) - Wood in U. 27. b. (inclusive) - U. 22. Central. On Left - a straight line from B. 17. a. 3. 6. to U. 21. Central. 1st objective - a Line from SONIA WOOD to PTE FOLIE FARM 2nd objective - (Bn. Objective) - U. 22. Central - S.E. exits of SERAIN. Battalion had by now been re-organized into 3 Companies. A, B & C. Companies.
8.10.18.	03.10 hrs.	Bn. left Quarry and TORRENS CANAL for forming up ground.
	04.10 hrs.	Bn. formed up as under.- C. Coy. (Right) A. Coy. (Left) on line -B.23.a.1.5. to B. 16. d. 4. 3. B. Coy. 500 yds. in rear with Bn. H.Q.
	05.10 hrs.	Advance commenced at zero hour. Battalion followed 9th Devons but considerable distance was made up and PONCHAUX was entered on heels of the Devons - In order to correct distances and check direction Battalion was halted in vicinity of B. 12. c. Central.
	08.03.hrs.	Battalion due to pass through 9th Devons on 1st objective No sign of Americans on Battalion Right - Attempts made to connect.
	08.10 hrs.	Battalion passed through 9th Devons.
	08.58 hrs.	Battalion crossed crest of spur in U. 26. Central - No touch on Right - 66th Division seen to be advancing towards SERAIN on our Left.
	09.40 hrs.	Objective gained - in touch with 66th Division on Left but No touch with Americans on Right - Troops seen advancing S.W. of PREMONT.
	09.50 hrs.	Armoured cars passed through our line - Cavalry approach SERAIN from S.W. Considerable M.G.fire from village.
	10.50 hrs.	Right flank exposed but covered by two platoons of 20th Manchester Regiment under Captain Nicholls.
	12.25 hrs.	Battalion disposed as follows:- Bn.H.Q. U. 26. b. 5.5. R.A.P. U. 26. d. 2. 2. 2 Companies in Line with posts at U. 22. c. 3.4. U. 22. Central. U. 21. b. 5. 4. Right Company U. 21. b. 0.5. U. 21. b. 3.3. - Left Company. 1 Coy.in Reserve in trench elements in U. 26 central.
	13.10 hrs.	PREMONT appears to have been captured by cavalry.
	14.45 hrs.	Right Company posts altered to conform with Americans. New positions U. 22. c. 3.5. - U. 21. d. 6. 9. Round SERAIN FARM. Bn.H.Q. moved to U. 26. d. 3.3. 20th Manchesters making a defensive flank along line of canal from U. 22. c. 3.5 to U. 27. b. 7. 5.
	16.50 hrs.	Touch obtained with Americans on our Right. Junction post U. 22. c. 3. 5.
	21.00 hrs.	B. Coy. put up into line to join with the Americans at U. 28. a. 9. 9. Following forward movement ordered by Brigade H.Q. to conform with 66th Division on our Left - 2 posts each of 1 platoon pushed out to vicinity of U. 16. b. and d. respectively to make touch with 66th Division who were to establish themselves on high ground in U. 9 - U.10 c & d. U. 16. b. No touch was made with 66th Division and posts withdrew to our own line. Post was also pushed out to MARCH COPSE.

Date.	Hour.	Narrative.
9.10.18	05.20 hrs.	75th Brigade passed through Bn. Front Line.
	07.30 hrs.	Battalion concentrated in U. 21. d.
	08.29 hrs.	Divisional Commander ordered Battalion to proceed to U. 12. c. 95. 40. thence to Quarry at P. 33. c. 8. 9.
	12.35 hrs.	Battalion disposed as follows.- Bn.H.Q. & 2. Companies Sunken Road P. 33. c. 8. 2. 1 Company in Quarry at P. 33. c. 8. 9. Here it was found that a gap existed between Brigades from P. 34. a. 2.9. to P. 34. c. 0.7. I undertook to fill in this gap and attack over it in conjunction with flanking units of the 74th & 75th Brigades. 75th Brigade appeared to be hung up by M.G. fire from Railway embankment. Battalion did not co-operate with the 74th & 75th Brigades who eventually resumed the advance at 14.00 hrs.
	16.45 hrs.	Touch made with Left American Post at V. 4. d. 7. 1.
	22.00 hrs.	Battalion withdrew from sunken road to TROUAUX SOLDATS.
10.10.18.	05.30 hrs.	Battalion advanced again. 800 yds. in rear of 20th Manchester Regiment. Battalion was in Reserve to 7th Bde.
	08.55 hrs.	Battalion reached high ground in P. 30. d. and halted as advance of 74th & 75th Brigades was checked. In touch with American Supports on Right - Bn.H.Q. at P. 30. d. 5.5.
	18.00 hrs.	Battalion withdrawn to Bank at P. 30. d. 7. 7. Stand to positions dug in P. 30. d. central.
11.10.18.		Battalion remained at Bank at P. 30. d. 7. 7.
	18.30 hrs.	Bn. ordered to withdraw to ELINCOURT.
	23.02 hrs.	Bn. reached ELINCOURT and was correctly billetted.

Strength on going into Line 4/10/18.- 18 Officers. 442 Other Ranks.

CASUALTIES.-

	Killed.	Wounded.	Missing.	D. of W.	Sick.
Officers.	3	7	Nil.	Nil.	Nil.
Other Ranks.	39	196	24	7	27
Prisoners (Estimated).	250				

Lieutenant Colonel,
Commanding 21st Bn. The MANCHESTER Regiment.

"Duplicate War Diary"

:- SPECIAL ORDER :-

The Divisional Commander has asked me to convey to all ranks his appreciation of their splendid work during recent operations. The Divisional Commander realises to the full all the circumstances under which attacks have been carried out and has told me that he considers the work and fighting carried out by the Battalion to have been of the very highest order and he remains confident that when the Battalion is called upon to fight again - all ranks will join in adding to the reputation and the fighting record of the 21st MANCHESTER Regiment.

16th OCTOBER, 1918.

Cyril Lanax Lieutenant Colonel,
Commanding, 21st (S) Bn. The MANCHESTER Regt.

C.O.

-: SPECIAL ORDER :-

I wish to call to the notice of all ranks the names of the undermentioned Officers, Warrant Officers, N.C.Os. and men who performed exceptionally fine work during the recent operations and to place on record my appreciation of the splendid services which they rendered:-

        Major H.W.WALKER, M.C.
        Captain E.F.ORGILL, M.C.
        Captain W.H.COX.
        Lieutenant T.J.REDHEAD, M.C.
        Lieutenant J.W.BELL, M.C.
        Second Lieutenant T.W.THURLEY.
        Second Lieutenant J.D.PRESTON.
        Second Lieutenant H.BRUNDRETT.
        Second Lieutenant D.A.BEST. i/c.Signals.
        Captain A.M.BAYNE, R.A.M.C.

No. 1. Company.		No. 2. Coy.		H.Q.Coy.	
18729 C.S.M.Smith	"C"	19226 Sgt.Palin.	"B"	18826 C.S.M.Brownson.	
14281 L/C.Schofield	"C"	200320 Sgt.Longson	"B"	18669 Cpl.Mosley.	
252570 Pte.Teare	"C"	40645 Pte.Mason	"B"	19289 L/C.Wilcox.	
51649 Pte.Collins	"C"	8779 Pte.Kay	"B"	203116 Pte.Russell.	
19729 Pte.Schofield	"C"	51745 L/C.Shaw	"B"	54656 Pte.Buck	
9408 Pte.Hawthorne	"C"	26903 Pte.Orrell	"B"	44176 Pte.Holding.	
252542 Pte.Roberts	"C"	36076 Pte.Crosshand	"B"	19701 Pte.Rutter.	
43626 Pte.Birtles	"C"	252589 Pte.Leaver	"B"	19783 Pte.Harty.	
40590 Sgt.Fairhurst	"A"	19442 C.S.M.Lucy	"D"		
18608 Sgt.Haywood	"A"	23178 Sgt.Fenge	"D"		
203704 Pte.Highfield	"A"	51647 L/C.Coggan	"D"		
55055 L/C.Goodes	"A"	379802 Pte.Hilton	"D"		
302657 Cpl.Houldsworth	"A"	11190 Pte.Hickson	"D"		
245479 Cpl.Sellery	"A"	43653 Pte.Fletcher	"D"		
203055 Pte.Ward	"A"	24808 Sgt.Cooling	"D"		
252632 Pte.Evans	"A"	17271 Pte.Wood	"D"		

Battalion Details.
Captain H. INGHAM.   2/Lt:A.J.LIDDIARD.
43460 Cpl.Drummond.
54557 Pte.Thorniey.

and Bearer Squad from 77th Field Ambulance.

17th OCTOBER, 1918.   Lieutenant Colonel,
                                      Commanding, 21st Bn. The MANCHESTER Regiment.

21st (S) Battalion The Manchester Regiment.

NARRATIVE of Operations from 19th - 24th
OCTOBER, 1918.

REF. MAP. FRANCE. SHEET 57b.

19th. The Battalion moved up via ST. BENIN and relieved Left
Company of 1st/5th Gloucester Regiment in the BASUEL
Sector with No.1 Company in front line from R. 1. c. 9.
3. to R. 2. c. 3. 3. No.2 Company in Reserve at
Q. 12. d. Battalion H.Q. Q. 11. d. 8. 4. Relief complete
21.00 hrs.

20th.. Battalion Headquarters moved up to BASUEL R. 7. b. 8. 9.
07.00hrs. In accordance with orders received on 19th Second Lieut.
J.D.PRESTON with three patrols of eight men each advanced
under a barrage in conjunction with 20th Manchesters on
Left, 1st/5th Gloucesters on Right to make good the line
of RICHEMONT RIVER. The Battalion objective MILL at
R. 2. a. 1. 5. (exclusive) to R. 2. b. 15. 25. Objective
gained with over 50 prisoners and 5 machine guns, at
08.20 hrs. 1 platoon of No.2 Company sent out to
consolidate.
Troops on Left failing to reach objective, defensive flank
was formed with third platoon of No.2 Company. Company
Headquarters being established at R. 2. c. 2. 7. Line
held was R. 1. d. 3. 7. - R. 1. b. 9. 4. to R. 2. b.
15. 25. in touch with troops on Right.
Posts established on Northern side of RICHEMONT RIVER.
18.00hrs. Took over front as far as R. 2. d. 6. 4. from 1st/5th
Gloucester Regiment.

21st. Orders received for 25th Division to attack on a Brigade
frontage. 7th Brigade to take 1st objective, running
as follows:- L. 33. d. 3. 1. -FORRESTERS HOUSE L. 27. d.
2. 9. - North East edge of POMMEREUIL - extreme West
corner of wood - L. 20. d. 4. 5. Battalion on Right of
Brigade with objective L. 33. d. 3. 1. to L. 27. d. 3.3.
Day spent in preparation.

22nd. Preparation for attack continued.
22.30hrs. Posts withdrawn to line R. 8. b. 25. 85. along line of
Light Railway to junction of track R. 7. b. 20. 45.90
exclusive to enable line to conform with barrage arrangements.

23rd. 00.30hrs. Battalion formed up disposed as follows:-
No. 1. Company on Right. No. 2. Coy. on Left.
each with two platoons in Front Line and one in Reserve.
01.20hrs. Advance commenced at zero hour. Owing to heavy enemy
gas shelling and ground mist great difficulty was
experienced in keeping touch and direction, with the
result that the progress of the attack was for a long
time uncertain.
02.40hrs. (Captain J.H.MILLER, M.C.) on Right) reported attack held
up owing to a large amount of wire and very heavy enemy
machine gun fire.
05.20hrs. Objective reported taken with assistance of a tank.
This report was found to be an error as line was
subsequently discovered to be from 200 - 300 yards short
of objective. Consolidation took place on this line.
05.05hrs. Patrols sent out to obtain touch on left and right.
11.00hrs. Touch obtained with 5th Division on Right.
18.00hrs. Orders received to form defensive flank - right Divisional
boundary L. 33. d. 5. 3. to L. 28. d. 3. 2.
22.30hrs. Defensive flank completed.

- 2 -

24th. 05.00 hrs. Orders received to withdraw troops to POMMEREUIL.
      09.40 hrs. Withdrawal complete.
      17.00 hrs. Orders received to attach No. 2. Company as Reserve Coy. to 20th Bn. The MANCHESTER Regiment.
      19.00 hrs. No. 1. Company and H.Q. in Brigade Reserve. Company H.Q. L. 12. c. Battalion H.Q. L. 11.c. 5. 2.

STRENGTH on going into the line:- 9 Officers. 308 Other Ranks.

Casualties.-

	Killed.	Wounded.	Missing.	D. of W.	Sick.
Officers.	-	2	-	-	-
Other Ranks.	6	69	13	-	8
Prisoners (estimated).	150.				

31/10/18.

Gerald Muir

Major,
Commanding 21st Bn. The MANCHESTER Regiment.

Reinforcements for the Month of October 1918.

```
13-10-18.    -      112  Other Ranks
14-10-18.    -        6    "      "
21-10-18.   3 Off.   31    "      "
24-10-18.   1        98    "      "
25-10-18.   -        99    "      "
28-10-18.   2        -
29-10-18.   -         3    "      "
30-10-18.   -         2    "      "
```

Casualties for the Month of October 1918

3/11-10-18.

	KILLED	WOUNDED	MISSING	D of W
Officers	3	7	Nil	Nil
ORs.	39	196	24	7

19/24-10-18.

	KILLED	WOUNDED	MISSING	D of W
Officers	-	2	-	-
ORs.	6	69	13	

25/29-10-18

	KILLED	WOUNDED	MISSING	D of W
Officers	-	2	-	
ORs.	-	19	-	

S E C R E T.   COPY NO. 41

75th INFANTRY BRIGADE INSTRUCTIONS NO.1 - Series "A".

Ref. map 1/40,000 Sheets 57A & 57B.   31/10/18.

1.   On a date and at an hour to be notified later, an operation on a large scale will be carried out, with a view to breaking through the enemy defences.

2.   OBJECTIVES AND BOUNDARIES.

(a)   The objectives allotted to 25th Division, the inter Divisional and inter Battalion boundaries of 75th Inf. Bde. are shown on attached map (Battalions only).

(b)   The objectives of 25th Division are :-
1st objective - RED LINE.
    The spur on which LANDRECIES is situated, defined as follows :-
    G.23.c.0.3 - Road junc: G.23.c.8.4 - Road junc:
    G.23.d.25.85 - Road junc: G.23.b.6.3 - point on canal
    G.17.d.9.8 (on existing bridge).
2nd objective - GREEN LINE.
    H.17.d.7.8 - RUE DU FAUX - RUE DES SABLONNIERES -
    RUE DES JUIFS (all villages inclusive) to Canal at
    B.27.d.75.35.

(c)   Right Divisional Boundary.
    G.20.central - G.22.central - G.23.c.8.4 - G.23.d.8.0 - thence MAROILLES Road (inclusive) as far as H.16.d.0.6, and thence a straight line to H.17.d.8.6.

Left Divisional Boundary.
G.8.d.7.7 - in straight line to Road junc: G.16.a.9.7 (incl.) - point on Railway G.17.b.2.1 - Canal at G.17.d.8.7 (inclusive of bridge at that point - thence Canal (exclusive).

        G.16.d.55.35
(inclusive to Northern Bn.)
From here to the canal, Boundaries will overlap.

Gloucesters. Road and Railway crossing G.16.d.7.3 - along road to bridge G.23.a.30.85.

Warwicks. Road and Railway crossing G.16.d.7.3 - along road to G.23.a.1.7.

(d)   Details as regards identity and tasks of Inf. Bdes. on Right and Left of 75th Inf. Bde. will be issued as soon as known.

3.   FORMING UP LINE.

    Approximate forming up line will be G.20.b.4.8 - G.8.d.7.7. This is liable to alteration as soon as the opening line of the barrage has been decided on.

4.   METHOD OF CARRYING OUT ATTACK.

(a)   The 75th Inf. Bde. will capture the 1st objective (RED LINE); the 74th Inf. Bde. will pass through 75th Inf. Bde. and capture 2nd objective (GREEN LINE). The 7th Inf. Bde. will be in Divisional Reserve.

(b)   (i) The main object of the 75th Inf. Bde. is to cross the SAMBRE Canal and establish a bridge head to admit of troops pressing on South of the canal. When this bridge head has been established on the RED LINE, 75th Inf. Bde. will push forward an Outpost Line on the line G.29.a.0.0 - G.29.central - G.30.b.0.9 - H.19.a.5.0 - H.13.d.0.0.

(ii)/....

S E C R E T.   COPY NO. 61

75th INFANTRY BRIGADE INSTRUCTIONS NO.1 - Series "A".

Ref. map 1/40,000 Sheets 57A & 57B.   31/10/18.

1. On a date and at an hour to be notified later, an operation on a large scale will be carried out, with a view to breaking through the enemy defences.

2. OBJECTIVES AND BOUNDARIES.

   (a) The objectives allotted to 25th Division, the inter Divisional and inter Battalion boundaries of 75th Inf. Bde. are shown on attached map (Battalions only).

   (b) The objectives of 25th Division are :-
   1st objective - RED LINE.
        The spur on which LANDRECIES is situated, defined as follows :-
        G.23.c.0.3 - Road junc: G.23.c.8.4 - Road junc:
        G.23.d.25.85 - Road junc: G.23.b.6.3 - point on canal G.17.d.9.8 (on existing bridge).
   2nd objective - GREEN LINE.
        H.17.d.7.8 - RUE DU FAUX - RUE DES SABLONNIERES - RUE DES JUIFS (all villages inclusive) to Canal at B.27.d.75.35.

   (c) Right Divisional Boundary.
   G.20.central - G.22.central - G.23.c.8.4 - G.23.d.8.0 - thence MAROILLES Road (inclusive) as far as H.16.d.0.6, and thence a straight line to H.17.d.8.6.

   Left Divisional Boundary.   point on railway G.17.b.21
                                                  Canal at G.17.d.87
   G.8.d.7.7 - in straight line to road junc: G.16.a.9.7 (incl.) - (inclusive of bridge at that point - thence Canal (exclusive).

   Inter Battalion Boundary.
   Track junc: G.15.a.05.20 - Road junc: G.16.d.55.35 (inclusive to Northern Bn.)
   From here to the canal, Boundaries will overlap.

   Gloucesters. Road and Railway crossing G.16.d.7.3 - along road to bridge G.23.a.30.85.

   Warwicks. Road and Railway crossing G.16.d.7.3 - along road to G.23.a.1.7.

   (d) Details as regards identity and tasks of Inf. Bdes. on Right and Left of 75th Inf. Bde. will be issued as soon as known.

3. FORMING UP LINE.

   Approximate forming up line will be G.20.b.4.8 - G.8.d.7.7. This is liable to alteration as soon as the opening line of the barrage has been decided on.

4. METHOD OF CARRYING OUT ATTACK.

   (a) The 75th Inf. Bde. will capture the 1st objective (RED LINE); the 74th Inf. Bde. will pass through 75th Inf. Bde. and capture 2nd objective (GREEN LINE).   The 7th Inf. Bde. will be in Divisional Reserve.

   (b) (i) The main object of the 75th Inf. Bde. is to cross the SAMBRE Canal and establish a bridge head to admit of troops pressing on South of the canal. When this bridge head has been established on the RED LINE, 75th Inf. Bde. will push forward an Outpost Line on the line G.29.a.0.0 - G.29.central - G.30.b.0.9 - H.19.a.5.0 - H.13.d.0.0.

(ii)/....

(2)

(ii) The attack as far as the canal will be carried out by the 1/5th Bn. Gloucestershire Regt. on the Right and 1/8th Bn. Royal Warwickshire Regt. on the Left. Each Battalion on a two Company front. The 1/8th Bn. Worcestershire Regt. will follow up the attack of the other two Battalions and will be responsible for forcing the passage of the Canal and establishing first the RED LINE, and secondly the Outpost Line, detailed above. These instructions will not preclude the two leading Battalions forcing the passage of the CANAL if feasible. In the latter case, these two Battalions will provide covering parties on the Southern bank of the Canal, who will enable the 1/8th Bn. Worcestershire Regt. to cross the river, and pass through them on to the RED LINE.

(c) The 74th Inf. Bde. will push through 75th Inf. Bde. at about ZERO plus 7 hours.

5. ARRANGEMENTS FOR CROSSING CANAL.

(a) The leading troops to reach the Canal will at once make for, and endeavour to save from demolition, the crossing known to exist over the Canal. R.E. will be detailed to accompany those Infantry parties to whom this special task is allotted.

Case I (one or more bridges found fit for use).

(i) Should any bridge be found to be fit for use, word must be sent back at once to the *Brigade* and to the R.E. Officer on the spot who is in charge of the bridging operation.

(ii) The Infantry must push across at once and establish themselves on the far bank of the Canal, so as to protect the particular crossing which has been made good.

(iii) Other troops will also be sent forward to make use of the crossing, or crossings, which have been then seized, with a view to establishing themselves along the whole of the S.E. bank of the canal within the Divisional boundaries, and within the protective barrage which will stand for one hour on a line parallel to and 300 yards S.E. of the Canal bank.

(iv) The R.E. who accompany the advanced infantry will be responsible for withdrawing any unexploded charges from the bridges.

Case II (all existing crossings destroyed or unfit for horse transport.

Full use must be made of covering fire by those troops not actually engaged in the crossing to keep down the fire of the defenders, who may be expected to shoot from the ramparts and houses on the Northern, Western, and Southern outskirts of LANDRECIES.

(b) The C.R.E. is arranging for the construction of rafts to convey 75th Inf. Bde. across the Canal. Practice in the use of these rafts will be carried out by the troops who will have to use them, and the R.E. personnel to be employed, under instructions to be issued later.

(c) Life belts and life lines are being obtained for the use of the 75th Inf. Bde.

(d) Officers and Other Ranks of 1/8th Bn. Worcestershire Regt. will be equipped as lightly as possible – puttees will not be worn. The 1/8th Bn. Royal Warwickshire Regt. and 1/5th Bn. Gloucestershire Regt. will similarly equip special parties whose duty will be to cross the Canal if possible as soon as these Battalions reach it, as detailed in para. 4 (b) (ii) above.

(e)/....

(3)

(e) Arrangements will be made to send up dry clothes and rum as early as possible after the bridges across the Canal have been constructed.

6. LIGHT SIGNALS.

The following "Success" Signals will be used by the Infantry :-

When leading troops have crossed Canal, – Three White lights.
When RED LINE reached, – Three Red lights.

These Signals are being obtained and will be issued as follows :-

	White.	Red.
1/8th Bn. Royal Warwickshire Regt.	12.	–
1/5th Bn. Gloucestershire Regt.	12.	–
1/8th Bn. Worcestershire Regt.	26.	50.

The two leading Battalions will not fire the White lights unless they have crossed the river in sufficient numbers to carry out their task as detailed in para.4 (b) (ii) above.

7. ARTILLERY.

(a) The Artillery supporting the attack of the 25th Division will be :-
   4 Brigades Field Artillery.
   1 Brigade Heavy Artillery.
In addition a proportion of the Corps Heavy Artillery will fire on selected targets on the Divisional front.

(b) The Infantry attack will be made under a creeping barrage moving forward at the rate of 100 yards in 6 minutes.

(c) Further instructions regarding the Artillery action will be issued later.

8. MACHINE GUNS.

(a) The machine guns available to support the attack will be :-
   25th Bn. Machine Gun Corps) under command of O.C. 25th
   1 Coy. 100th Bn. M.G.C.   ) Bn. M.G.C.

(b) Machine guns will be required to carry out the following tasks :-
   (i) To cover the advance of 75th Inf. Bde. by firing machine gun barrages. When they can no longer fire from their original positions, a proportion of machine guns will be moved forward to new positions to cover the crossing of the Canal.

   (ii) To protect the right flank of 75th Inf. Bde. during its advance to the Canal.

(c) Three Sections Machine Guns will be attached to 75th Inf. Bde. to assist in consolidation of RED LINE. These will fire in the opening barrages.

9. TANKS.

(a) 2 tanks will be attached to each of the leading Battalions to co-operate with them in their advance to the Canal. The primary objectives of these tanks will be the enemy front line system. After the enemy's resistance here has been overcome, the 2 tanks on the left will proceed just North of the FONTAINE AU BOIS - LANDRECIES Road to the Railway at G.16.d.6.3. Those on the right will proceed South following the line of the Light Railway in G.15.b, and d to where it joins the main line at G.22.a.0.2. Thence they will proceed N.E. along the main line to G.16.d.6.3. From here onwards all four tanks will make

every/....

every endeavour to assist the Infantry crossing the Canal by the provision of covering fire from the N.W. bank.

(b) Three Infantry carrying tanks will also be available and will be used to carry a party of Infantry (42 all ranks) and 6 R.E's direct to the LANDRECIES Bridge without regard to the pace of the barrage or other considerations, in the hope that they will reach the bridge before it has been demolished. Further instructions on this matter will be issued later.

10. TRENCH MORTARS.

Two Sections 6" Newton Trench Mortars will follow close behind the Infantry to co-operate by firing at machine gun emplacements on the S.E. bank of the Canal, and providing covering fire during the crossing of the leading Infantry Battalion.
In addition, a single gun section of the 75th L.T.M. Battery will be attached to each Battalion.

11. SMOKE.

Smoke screens will be provided by the Artillery, No. I Special Company R.E., and by aeroplanes, to cover the advance of the Infantry from observation from the South. Further particulars regarding this will be issued.

12. ROADS.

In the first instance the line of advance of the Division will be as follows :-
POMMEREUIL - CHAPEL Cross Roads L.29.a.3.2 - MALGARNI - Road Junc: L.18.c.7.8 - Road junc: G.19.b.7.9 - G.14.c.3.4 - G.20.b.0.6 G.16.d.6.4.
C.R.E. will make a track from L.24.a.4.8 - G.20.b.0.6 fit for limbers, in order that MALGARNI may be avoided.

13. COMMUNICATIONS.

The truck line of communication will be the same as the line of advance (see para.12).

14. Headquarters of 75th Inf. Bde. at ZERO will be in MALGARNI, exact location will be notified later.

15. ACKNOWLEDGE.

Cunningham
Major,
for Brigade Major, 75th Infantry Brigade.

Issued through Signals at 20.00 hrs

Copies to:
1. 1/8th R.Warwick Regt.
2. 1/5th Gloucester Regt.
3. 1/8th Worcester Regt.
4. L.T.M. Battery.
5. 7th Inf. Bde.
6. 74th Inf. Bde.
7. 25th Div. 'G'.
8. 330th Bde. R.F.A.
9. 25th Bn. M.G.C.
10. 'C' Coy. 9th Bn. Tank Corps.
11. 76th Field Amb.
12. Staff Captain.
13. Signals.
14. War Diary.
15. " "
16.- 19. Retained.

Army Form C. 2118.

WAR DIARY
or
INTELLIGENCE SUMMARY.

Instructions regarding War Diaries and Intelligence Summaries are contained in F.S. Regs., Part II. and the Staff Manual respectively. Title pages will be prepared in manuscript.

21st (S) Battalion The ~~Brass Grading our Regiment~~. November, 1918. Volume 57.

Place	Date	Hour	Summary of Events and Information	Remarks and references to Appendices
LE CATEAU.	1		In Billets. Cleaning up. Fine.	
do	2		do Training. Showery.	
In the Line.	3		A. & C. Companies attached to 75th Infantry Brigade. B,D & H.Q. Companies moved to bivouacks L.27 d. B Echelon remained at Le Cateau. Fair.	
do	4		Battalion less A & C Coys moved to MAREGARNI 1415 hrs. A & C Coys rejoined Battalion 1700 hrs. Bn. moved to G 21 a & b. about this time. B Echelon left Le Cateau 1650 hrs for bivouacks in vicinity of POMMEREUIL. WET.	
do	5		Bn. advancing. Route. LANDRECIES—MAROILLES—BASSE NOYELLE. B Echelon moved at 1230 hrs to Landrecies area. In billets 1900 hrs. Wet.	
do	6		Bn. in Reserve Line advancing. At 1715 hrs. in vicinity of TAISNIERS. B Echelon moved to NORIOLLES. In billets 1900 hrs. Wet.	
do	7		Bn. found Advance Guard for the Brigade. B Echelon moved to TAISNIERES. All in billets 1430 hrs. Fair.	
DOMPIERRE.	8		Bn. relieved by 5th Inniskillings 0018 hrs.In billets DOMPIERRE. Fine.	
MAROILLES.	9		Bn. left DOMPIERRE for MAROILLES. B Echelon left TAISNIERES for MAROILLES. Whole of Battalion in billets 1630 hrs. Fine.	
LANDRECIES.	10		Bn left for LANDRECIES. In billets 1300 hrs. Fine.	
do	11		In Billets. Cleaning up. Fine. (Armistice at 1100hrs)	
do	12		do Training. Fine.	
POMMEREUIL.	13		Bn. left LANDRECIES 1100hrs. In billets at POMMEREUIL 1445hrs. Fine.	
do	14		do do do	
do	15		do Fine.	
do	16		do do	
do	17		do Fair, Tents much.	
do	18		do Fine, training and salvage work.	
do	19		do do is do the	
do	20		do do do	
do	21		do do do	
do	22		do do do	
do	23		do do the	
do	24		do do do	
do	25		do do training, bathe & salvage do	
do	26		do do do	
do	27		do do do	

Army Form C. 2118.

WAR DIARY
or
INTELLIGENCE SUMMARY.

(Erase heading not required.)

21st (S) Bn., The Manchester Regiment.

November 1918.

Place	Date	Hour	Summary of Events and Information	Remarks and references to Appendices
...	28		billets. ... no silver band. ...	
do			inera'n left for QUIEVY.	
QUIEVY	30		ing.	

Reinforcements & Casualties attached.

Christian
..den Lt Colonel.
Comdg. 21st Bn. The Manchester Regt.

WAR DIARY
for
Month of November 1918.

CONTENTS.

1. War Diary.

APPENDICES.

Appendix. 1.   Narrative of Operations.

Appendix. 1a. Narrative of Operations of A. and C. Companies.

Appendix. 2.   Brigade Operation Orders of 7th and 75th Infantry Brigades in sequence.

Appendix. 3.   Battalion Operation Orders in sequence.

Appendix. 4.   Messages sent and received during Operations 3/8-11-18.

2nd December, 1918.

Chudanax

Lieut:Colonel,
Commanding 21st Bn; The Manchester Regiment.

INSTRUCTION No. in connection
with move of Bn. to-day.
21st Battalion the MANCHESTER Regiment. 5/11/18.

Ref. Maps. 1/20,000 YUNAS.

1. Battalion (less A & C. Coys) will move from present area to vicinity of FRESNEAU to-day. On arrival Battalion (less A & C. Coys) will bivouac. No bivouacs will be erected before dusk.

2. Detail for the move:-
   Starting Point.- STATION factor M.
   Time.- 15.00 hrs.
   Order of march.- H. , B & D. Coys.
   Usual distances will be maintained.

3. Companies will be completely equipped for battle before moving off.

4. ACKNOWLEDGE.

   C.J.Hepp
   Lieutenant & A/Adjutant,
   Issued at BY PUNCH. 21st Bn. The Manchester Regiment.

To all recipients of Operation Orders.

SPECIAL ORDER:-

I wish to congratulate Major MACKAY and all ranks under his command on the splendid results of the recent fighting. The Battalion has once more distinguished itself in active operations and the fighting reputation of the Regiment has been enhanced by the recent victory. I commend all ranks for the splendid perseverance and courage shown throughout a very trying period of battle.

I wish to place on record my great appreciation of the splendid work carried out by all ranks. The following Officers, W.Os, N.C.Os. and men have earned special mention and I wish to call the attention of all ranks to the example which they have set to their comrades:-

Captain E.F. ORGILL, M.C.
Captain J.H. MILLER, M.C.
Second Lieutenant J.D. PRESTON.
Second Lieutenant D.A. BEST.
Second Lieutenant H.P. BRUMMITT.

H. Coy.
A/R.S.M. Brownson H.
L/C. Armstrong S.
L/C. Willcock R.
Pte. Sutter A.E.
Pte. Holding W.J.
Pte. Whitehead A.
Pte. Russell J.
Pte. Lee H.

No. 1 Coy.
Sgt. Hayward E.
Sgt. Smith H.
Sgt. Alderdice J.
Cpl. Mouldsworth J.
Sgt. Featherstone E.
Cpl. Sollery L.B.
Pte. Knowles A.
Pte. Deans W.
Pte. Wood S. (45646)
Pte. Lawson A.
Pte. Ward W.E.
Pte. Jackson J.
Pte. Ross H.

No. 2 Coy.
Sgt. Crossland J.
Sgt. Wilkinson C.
Cpl. Toft J.
Pte. Shepherd C.
Cpl. Alcock W.P.
Pte. Pritchard R.
Pte. Kingsley W.
Pte. Parry S.
Pte. Matthews C.
Pte. Smith W.K.
Pte. Fletcher J.
xxx.

3/11/18.

Lieutenant Colonel
Commanding 21st Bn. Manchester Regiment

SECRET.   COPY NO. 21

Bull Hooks

75th INFANTRY BRIGADE INSTRUCTIONS NO.2 - SERIES "A".

Ref. map 1/40,000 Sheets 57A & 57B.   2/11/18.

1. **OBJECTIVES.**
   The 1st objective RED LINE, has now been altered to run as follows :-
   G.23.c.0.0 - Hill at G.23.c.5.0 - along Road to Road junc:
   G.23.d.25.85 - Road junc: G.23.b.6.3 - Point on Canal
   G.17.d.9.8 (on existing bridge) - G.17.b.6.0.

2. **INTER BATTALION BOUNDARY.**
   The Inter Battalion Boundary given in Instructions No.1 Series "A" will be continued from LANDRECIES Bridge along Light Railway to G.23.d.1.8.

3. **FLANK FORMATIONS.**
   149th Inf. Bde. is attacking on the left of the 75th Inf. Bde. The Right Battalion of this Brigade will be 3rd Royal Fusiliers, H.Q., G.7.b.3.0.
   96th Inf. Bde. is attacking on the right of the 75th Inf. Bde. The Left Battalion of this Brigade will be *16th Lancs Fus.*

4. **MOVE OF 1/8th BN. WORCESTERSHIRE REGT. & POSITION OF BATTN. H.Q. AT ZERO.**
   1/8th Bn. Worcestershire Regt. will move into assembly positions from POMMEREUIL on Y/Z night.
   Battalion H.Q. at ZERO will be :-
   1/8th Bn. Royal Warwickshire Regt.   = G.14.a.25.75.
   1/5th Bn. Gloucestershire Regt.)
   1/8th Bn. Worcestershire Regt.   )   = G.20.a.6.8.

5. **ACTION ON RIGHT FLANK.**
   (a) 96th Inf. Bde. intend to make good the Spur in G.20.d, G.27.a, on November 2nd.
   (b) On 'Z' day 32nd Division will mop up South of the Grid line *running* East and West through G.20.central, G.21.central, as far as South and South-east as the River.
   (c) 2 Companies 21st Bn. Manchester Regt. of 7th Inf. Bde. *have been* placed under the orders of G.O.C., 75th Inf. Bde, to mop up the area between the right flank of 75th Inf. Bde. during its advance (i.e., the line G.20.b.4.8 - G.22.a.0.0) and the Grid line through G.20.central, G.21.central.
   Further instructions will be issued as regards this as soon as it has been determined to what extent the attack of the 96th Inf. Bde. on November 2nd has been successful.

6. **LIAISON POSTS.**
   Liaison posts will be established as under :-
   1/8th Bn. Worc. Regt & 3rd Bn. R.F. (149th Bde.)   On RED LINE
                                                      (G.17.b.7.0.
   1/8th Bn. Worc. Regt & *16th Lancs Fus* (96th Bde.) On RED LINE at
                                                      G.22.b.5.0 &
                                                      G.23.c.0.2.
   21st Manchester Regt. & *16th Lancs Fus* (96th Bde.) On road at
                                                      G.21.b.4.0.
                                                      On railway G.22.a.0.0

   In addition to above 1/8th Bn. R. Warwickshire Regt. during its advance will gain touch with 3rd Bn. R.F. (149th Bde.) at G.10.c.85.10.

                                                          7/.......

(2)

7. ACTION OF 1/8th BN. WORCESTERSHIRE REGT. AFTER SECURING RED LINE.
After securing the RED LINE, O.C., 1/8th Bn. Worcestershire Regt. will not weaken that line by pushing troops forward on to the Outpost Line, until he ensures himself that at least one Company each of the 1/8th Bn. R.Warwickshire Regt. and the 1/5th Bn. Gloucestershire Regt. have crossed the Canal and have occupied positions from which they can reinforce the RED LINE if necessary. The latter two Battalions will therefore make every endeavour to push their men across the Canal as expeditiously as possible after the 1/8th Bn. Worcestershire Regt. have passed through them.

8. ARTILLERY.
The starting line of the creeping barrage will be G.20.b.4.0 - G.9.c.1.6.
The timing of the barrage will be as follows :-
Lifts from starting line.   ZERO plus 4 minutes.

Barrage moves forward at the rate of 100 yds. in 6 mins.)
Protective barrage formed 300 yds. S.E. of and parallel)
to Canal, standing for 60 mins. after most Northerly)
point is formed.)

Barrage lifts from protective barrage
and Infantry advance.   ZERO plus 4 hours, 18 mins.

Barrage moves forward at rate of 100 yds. in 6 mins.)
until protector 300 yds. S.E. of RED LINE is reached.)

Infantry advance from RED LINE
to take up Outpost Line.   ZERO plus 5 hours, 30 mins.

9. ACTION OF MACHINE GUNS.
The tasks of the 25th Bn. M.G.C. include the following :-
Task (i). To assist the original attack of the 75th Inf. Bde. by barraging selected targets.
Task (ii). To produce intense covering fire on to the ground S.E. of the Canal and on to the Western outskirts on LANDRECIES during the period that the Infantry are crossing the Canal.
Task (iii). To assist the 75th Inf. Bde. in the consolidation of the RED LINE.

For this operation the 25th Bn. M.G.Corps will be reinforced by one Company of the 100th Bn. M.G.Corps.
The above tasks will be carried out as follows :-
Task (i). The original barrage will be carried out by :-
1 Coy. 100th Bn. M.G.C.   16 M.G's.
"A" Coy. 25th Bn. M.G.C.   12   "
"B" Coy.(less 1 section)   8   "
"C" Coy.   12   "
                            Total   48

These guns will be in positions along the general line G.13.d.6.0 - G.14.a.0.0 - G.8.c.0.0, to fire on targets in the area G.21.b, G.21.c, G21.d, G.15.b and d, and G.16.a. and c.
2 Sections of "A" Coy. 25th Bn. M.G.C. will be in position about the Infantry forming up line, and will open fire as soon as possible after ZERO on the bridge in G.23.a to prevent this being blown up by the enemy.

Task (ii). Covering fire during Canal crossing will be provided as follows :-
(a)   1 section "B" Coy. 25th Bn. M.G.C. will advance immediately behind the Infantry and will take up commanding position in the houses on N.E. bank of Canal in G.25.a so as to bring direct fire at close range on to the S.E. bank of the Canal in a South - westerly and North-easterly direction. This section will instantly engage any opposition to the crossing of the Canal that may come from the S.E. side.

(b)/......

(3)

(b) "C" Coy. 25th Bn.M.G.C. (12 guns) will move from original barrage positions at ZERO plus 45 mins. to positions at G.15.d.3.8 and will open fire at ZERO plus 1 hour 30 mins. on S.E. bank of Canal and N.W. outskirts of LANDRECIES in G.23.a. and G.22.b. and d. Direct fire will be employed if observation permits. If visibility renders direct fire impossible, indirect fire will be employed in accordance with artillery barrage time table. Guns will fire at as rapid a rate as possible while Infantry are crossing the Canal.

(c) "D" Coy. 25th Bn.M.G.C. will co-operate in providing covering fire during the crossing of the Canal as follows :-

  (i) 1 section will occupy positions in Railway Cutting about G.27.a.7.8 from which it will bring direct fire to bear on the area S.E. of the Canal in G.27.d - G.28.a during the advance to and the crossing of the Canal by the 75th Inf. Bde. It will also take any opportunity of engaging any defences on the Canal bank in G.22 by direct enfilade fire during the advance up to the Canal.

  (ii) 1 section will move as close as possible behind the Infantry to occupy positions in Railway Cutting about G.22.a.0.2 from which it will bring direct overhead fire on the area S.E. of the Canal G.22. and G.28.a during the advance to and crossing of the Canal by the 75th Inf. Bde.

  (iii) 1 section will move as close as possible behind the Infantry to occupy positions about G.17.d.2.8 from which it can bring direct fire on to the area S.E. of the Canal in G.17.d. and G.18.c

Task (iii). Defence of the RED LINE.
"B" Coy. 25th Bn. M.G.C. (less 1 section) on completion of original barrage at ZERO plus 1 hour 30 mins. will move forward as rapidly as possible to occupy positions on the flanks of the RED LINE in G.23.c and G.23.b. The remaining section of "B" Coy., covering the Canal crossing from houses on N.W. bank of Canal, will, on completion of their task, join the remainder of "B" Coy. and will take up positions in the centre of the RED LINE in G.23.d.

"B" Coy. 25th Bn.M.G.C. will be under the orders of G.O.C. 75th Inf. Bde. for the consolidation of the RED LINE.

10. SPECIAL ARRANGEMENTS FOR CROSSING THE SAMBRE CANAL.
(a) It is intended that in the case of destruction of the standing bridges the crossing of the Canal in the first instance should be made on petrol tin rafts, each raft being capable of carrying 1 man.

105th Field Coy.R.E. are responsible for the launching of these rafts and will be assisted by carrying parties found from 11th Bn. South Lancashire Regt.

Three dumps of rafts are being formed prior to ZERO at suitable places in rear of the front line to be selected by O.C. 105th Field Coy.R.E.

The raft personnel is being divided into parties of 15 men, each party with 5 rafts, and will be distributed as under :-

(i) 7 parties (35 rafts) to advance with the rear Companies of the 1/8th Bn.R.Warwickshire Regt. These will be responsible for the crossing of the Canal N.E. of LANDRECIES.

(ii) 5 parties (25 rafts) to advance with the rear Companies of 1/5th Bn.Gloucestershire Regt. These will be responsible for
  (a) The crossing and bridging of the stream in G.22.a, b and c. (15 rafts).
  (b) The crossing of the main Canal S.W. of LANDRECIES, in the event of it being possible for this Battalion to effect a crossing. (10 rafts).

(iii)/......

(iii) 4 parties (20 rafts) to accompany the Right Front Company of 1/8th Bn. Worcestershire Regt. These will be responsible for the passing of troops across the Canal S.W. of LANDRECIES in addition to those detailed in (ii) (b) above.

Raft parties during the advance will be under the command of the Battalion Commanders with whose Companies they are advancing. Battalion Commanders will select forming up lines for the parties who accompany their Battalions. These forming up lines will be pointed out to Officers concerned under arrangements wo be made between Battalion Commanders and O.C. 105th Field Coy.R.E.

In case of casualties during the advance Battalions will be prepared to give every assistance to the Royal Engineers to ensure that the largest possible number of rafts reach the Canal bank.

(b) A further carrying party with 2 light trussed bridges 22 ft. long will be supplied by 130th Field Coy.R.E. and will advance with the 1/5th Bn. Gloucestershire Regt. These bridges will be utilized for spanning the lock at LANDRECIES in the event of it being standing or only partially demolished.

This party will report to Battalion H.Q., 1/5th Bn. Gloucestershire Regt. (L.18.c.6.2) at 11.00 hours on "Y" day.

(c) Sappers from 182nd Tunnelling Coy. will be attached to Battalions as under :- They will be responsible for the cutting of leads and the withdrawal of demolition charges placed to destroy the bridges.

For bridge at.	No. of Sappers.	To be attached to.
LANDRECIES.	10.	1/5th Bn. Glouc Regt.
G.17.d.9.8.	5.	1/5th Bn. Glouc. Regt.
G.22.c.6.1) G.22.d.0.5)	5.	1/8th Bn.R.Warwick Regt.

These parties will report to Battalions at 11.00 hours on "Y" day.

(d) Two pontoon bridges are being constructed N.E. and S.W. of the LANDRECIES Bridge which will be available for Field Guns and Horse Transport at ZERO plus 7 hours.

11. TANKS.
(a) No Infantry carrying tanks are now available - para.9 (b), Instructions No.1 Series "A" is therefore cancelled.
(b) (i) The 4 tanks detailed in Instructions No.1. Series "A" para.9 (a) will be a composite section from 9th Tank Bn. known as I Section. They will be under the command of Lieut R.S. DALGLEISH, M.C.
(ii) The tank rallying point will be in valley about G.9.central or if the tactical situation does not permit of this, at the Tankodrome at L.15.c.
(iii) Tanks will cross the SAMBRE River and assist in operations on the N.E. side of it as soon as bridges are available to carry them, but no tank must attempt to cross the river by standing bridges unless they have been certified by the R.E. Officer on the spot as being able to bear them.

12. CO-OPERATION OF R.A.F. AND SMOKE.
The 35th Squadron R.A.F. will co-operate as follows :-
(a) Contact planes.
Contact planes will be provided to call for flares :-
(i) At ZERO plus 6 hours on RED LINE.
(ii) At ZERO plus 8 hours to verify (i) above.
(iii) At 14.00 hours and 16.00 hours between RED and GREEN LINES.

(b)/....

(5).

(b) <u>Counter-attack patrols</u>.
Counter-attack patrols will be kept up continuously in the air from ZERO to dusk. In the event of a counter-attack this plane will drop white parachute lights over the centre of the hostile troops.

<u>SMOKE</u>.
Arrangements have been made with 15th Wing R.A.F. to keep under smoke cloud the following areas :-
(i) Spur in H.14, 2o, 26, 27 and 33.
(ii) Spur in N.9, 10, 11 and 18.

The above areas will be smoked from ZERO plus 30 mins to ZERO plus 2 hours and 30 mins, and for a longer period if it is clear to the aeroplanes that the crossing of the Canal has not been assured.

13. <u>EQUIPMENT</u>.
A proportion of men in every platoon will carry bill-hooks.

14. <u>MEDICAL ARRANGEMENTS</u>.
At ZERO hour locations of Advanced Dressing Station, Vrelay posts, will be :-

Adv. Dressing Station   L.26.d.5.3. POMMEREUIL.
  (76th Field Amb.)

Relay Post & Adv. Car Post. MALGARNI.

15. ACKNOWLEDGE.

Major,
for Brigade Major, 75th Infantry Brigade.

Issued through Signals
  at

Copies: 1. 1/8th R. Warwick Regt.
        2. 1/5th Gloucester Regt.
        3. 1/8th Worcester Regt.
        4. L.T.M. Batty.
        5. 7th Inf. Bde.
        6. 74th Inf. Bde.
        7. 96th Inf. Bde.
        8. 149th Inf. Bde.
        9. 25th Div. 'G'.
       10. 33th Bde. R.F.A.
       11. 25th Bn. M.G.C.
       12. 'C' Coy. 9th Bn. Tank Corps.
       13. 76th Field Amb.
       14. 105th Field Coy. R.E.
       15. Staff Captain.
       16. Signals.
       17. War Diary.
       18. "   "
       19 - 20. Retained.

SECRET.   Copy No..........

7TH INFANTRY BRIGADE INSTRUCTIONS NO 1.

SERIES "E"

2nd November 1918.

Ref. Map. 1/20000. Sheet 57a N.W. and 57b N.E.

1.   The 25th Division with the 32nd Division on its right and 50th Division on its left will take part in an operation on a large scale, with a view to breaking through the enemies defences, on a date and at an hour to be notified later.

2.   Objectives and Boundaries of the Division are shown on the attached map "A".

3.   Forming up line will be approximately on the line G.20.b.4.8. – G.8.d.7.7., exact line will be notified as soon as the opening barrage has been fixed. Barrage line G.20.b.4.0. — G.9.c.1.6.

4.   (a)   The 75th Infantry Brigade will capture the first Objective (Red Line) and the outpost line beyond (Dotted Red). The 1/5th GLOUCESTERSHIRE REGT on the right and the 1/8th ROYAL WARWICKSHIRE REGT ON THE Left are attacking as far as the canal, the 1/8th Worcestershire Regt. is following up the attack, forcing the passage of the canal and establishing firstly the Red Line and then the outpost line beyond (Dotted Red). If practicable troops of the two leading Battalions will cross the canal first and form a covering party for the 1/8th Worcestershire Regt. whilst effecting the crossing

(b)   The 74th Infantry Brigade is pushing through the 75th Infantry Brigade at about Zero plus 7 hours (forcing the passage of the canal if the 74th Infantry Brigade has been unable to carry this out) and pushing on to the attack on the Green Line. The 11th SHERWOOD FORESTERS are carrying out this attack supported by the 9th YORKSHIRE REGT. The 13th DURHAM LIGHT INFANTRY will be in Brigade Reserve.

7th I. Bde will move to POMMEREUIL on Y day.

(c)   The 7th Infantry Brigade (less two companies 21st Manchester Regt.) is in Divisional Reserve. Two Companies 21st Manchester Regt under a senior officer will under orders of G.O.C. 75th Infantry Brigade be detailed to mop up the area between grid line through G.20.central – G.21. central and the right flank of the 75th Infantry Brigade during its advance (G.20.b.4.8. – G.22.a.0.0.) Liaison Posts will be established by these Companies with 32nd Division. at :- G.21.b.4.0. (on road) G.22.a.0.0. (on railway).   O.C. 21st Manchester Regt. will arrange direct with G.O.C. 75th Infantry Brigade all details necessary for the assembly and subsequent duties of these companies, submitting a copy of his orders to this office immediately.
Further orders will be issued for the move of the 7th Infantry Brigade.

5.   Arrangements for crossing the Canal and LA PETITE HELPE RIVER are being made by C.R.E. with G.O.C's 74th and 75th Infantry Brigades and consist of :- (a) attempts to save existing crossings from destruction by sending forward parties of infantry and R.E's to examine bridges if still intact and remove charges.
(b)   Provision of rafts for carrying Infantry
(c)   Repairs (if necessary) of existing bridges.
(d)   Construction of new bridges.

6.   Light Signals will be used as follows:-

2.

        Three White Lights   -   Leading Battalion has crossed canal.

        Three Red Lights   -   Red Line reached.

7.   Artillery supporting the attack consists of:-

   (a)   Four Brigades Field Artillery.
   (b)   One Brigade Heavy Artillery.
   (c)   A proportion of the Corps Heavy Artillery.

      A creeping barrage lifting 100 yards in six minutes will cover the advance.
      One Brigade Field Artillery will be attached to 74th Infantry Brigade for the advance to the GREEN LINE.

8.   Machine Guns available consist of:-

  (a) 25th Bn. Machine Gun Corps   ) Under O.C. 25th Bn.
     One Company 100th Battn. Machine Gun Corps) Machine Gun Corps.

  (b) Machine Guns will be required to carry out the following tasks:-
     (i) To cover the advance of 75th Infantry Brigade by firing machine gun barrages. When they can no longer fire from their original positions, a proportion of machine guns will be moved forward to new positions to cover the crossing of the canal.
     (ii) To protect the right flank of 75th Infantry Brigade during its advance to the canal.

  (c) Three sections machine guns will be attached to 75th Infantry Brigade to assist in consolidation of Red Line. These will fire in the opening barrages.

  (d) Three Sections Machine Guns will be attached to 74th Infantry Bde. to come under orders of G.O.C. 74th Infantry Brigade when that Brigade moves forward across the canal.

9.   Tanks will assist in the advance as follows :-

  (a) 2 Fighting Tanks 9th Bn. Tank Corps will accompany each of the two leading battalions of 75th Infantry Brigade.

  (b) Carrying Tanks will also be used, further information will be issued referring to these.

10.   Trench Mortars will co-operate two sections of 6" Newtons following close behind the infantry.

11.   Smoke screens will be provided by the Artillery - No 1. Special Company R.E. and by aeroplanes. Further particulars regarding this will be issued. R.A.F H.14.20.26 27 33
                                                                 4 9 10 11 18

12.   In the first instance the line of advance of the Division will be as follows :-
      POMMEREUIL - CHAPEL Cross Roads (L.29.a.3.2.) - MALGARNI - road junction L.18.c.7.8. - road junction on 4.19.b.7.9. - G.14.c.3.4. - G.20.b.0.6. - G.16.d.6.4.
      C.R.E. will make a track from L.24.a.4.8. - G.20.b.0.6. fit for limbers, in order that MALGARNI may be avoided.

13.   The Trunk line of communication will be the same as the line of advance.(see para 12.)

3.

14.   Headquarters at Zero will be:-

        Divisional Headquarters   - POMMEREUIL
        75th Infantry Brigade)
        74th Infantry Brigade)   - MALGARNI
        7th Infantry Brigade.   - POMMEREUIL.

ACKNOWLEDGE

                                        [signature]

                                        Captain.
                                Brigade Major, 7th Infantry Brigade.

Issued through signals at
........11.00....hours.

Copies to:-   1. 9th Bn. Devon Regt. *
               2. 20th Manchester Regt. *
               3. 21st Bn. Manchester Regt. *
               4. 7th L.T.M. Battery. *
               5. 74th Infantry Brigade.
               6. 75th Infantry Brigade.
               7. 25th Division "G"
               8. Bde. Signal Officer.
               9. Staff Captain.
              10. War Diary.
              11. File (2 copies)

        * Maps only issued to.

Un Ballo in Maschera

SECRET.

INSTRUCTIONS in connection with move of
the Battalion to-day.
––––––––––

3rd NOVEMBER, 1918.

In connection with the move of the Battalion to-day the following will be the arrangements:-

1. Usual billeting party from each Company under Captain W.H.COX will report to the Staff Captain at the Military Cemetery POMMEREUIL at 12.00 hrs.

2. Officers valises, surplus mess kit, blankets (rolled in bundles of ten) bone packs and overcoats will be stacked outside Q.M's stores by 11.00 hrs

3. The Transport Officer will detail 1 limber with two day's forage for the use of T.M.B. detachment, which will proceed with B & D Coys.

4. The following will be drawn:-
   (a) S.O.S.Grenades.- 1 per each platoon Headquarters, 3 per Coy. H.Q., 6 per Bn. H.Q.
   (b) 1 detonated bomb per man.
   (c) 1 extra bandolier per man.
   (d) Billhooks 10 per Coy.
   (e) Shovels 34 per Company.
   (f) Flares 1 per man.

5. (a) Lewis Gun Limbers will proceed with their Companies.
   (b) 1 Tool wagon will proceed with A & C. Coys and 1 with B & D. Coys.
   (c) 1 Cooker will proceed with A & C Coys. and 1 with B & D. Coys.
   1 will remain behind for details.
   The Cooker with A & C. Coys. will go as far as possible with these Coys. so that tea can be provided before these Coys. go into the line. This cooker will be under the orders of Captain J.H.MILLER, M.C.
   When A & C. Coys. have moved off this cooker will wait at POMMEREUIL Church for guide who will conduct it to the other half Battalion.
   1 Water Cart will proceed with B & D. Coys.

6. ACKNOWLEDGE.

Lieutenant & A/Adjutant,
Issued at   BY RUNNER.   21st Battalion The MANCHESTER Regiment.

To all recipients of Operation Orders.

S E C R E T.   Copy No..........

7TH INFANTRY BRIGADE INSTRUCTIONS NO 2.

SERIES "E"

Ref. Map. 1/20000, Sheets 57A N.W. and 57B N.E.

1. Reference para 3 Instructions No.1.

Barrage opens at Zero on the line G.20.b.4.0. - G.9.c.1.6.

2. Reference para 4 c Instructions No. 1.

(a) The 7th Infantry Brigade will move on Y day to bivouac in the vicinity of POMMEREUIL.

(b) Battalions will march to pass cross roads Q.4.b.4.0. at following times:-

 21st Manchester Regt. 15.50 hours.
 9th Devon Regt. 16.00 "
 20th Manchester Regt. 16.10 "
 7th L.T.M. Battery. 16.20 "

(c) Column to clear LE CATEAU by 17.00 hours and not to halt till clear of the town.

(d) Advance parties to receive areas and tents will meet Staff Captain at Military Cemetery POMMEREUIL at 13.00 hours.

(e) Transport Lines will not move for the present.

(f) Tents and bivouac shelters will not be erected until dusk.

(g) Brigade Headquarters will open at POMMEREUIL at a place and time to be notified later.

3. Reference para 9 b Instructions No 1.

4 Supply Tanks are moving forward under 75th Infantry Brigade carrying sappers and Infantry with Bridging material to save the existing bridges or erect new ones at the earliest possible moment.

4. Reference para 11 Instructions No. 1.

Smoke clouds will be formed by 15 Wing R.A.F. on following areas

 1. Spur in H.14, 20, 26, 27, and 33
 11 Spur in H. 9, 10, 11, and 18.

from Zero plus 30 minutes to plus 2 hours 30 minutes or longer if required.

5. Armoured Cars consisting of one Battery (7 cars) have been allotted to the XIII Corps.

2.

6. R.A.F. will co-operate by

(a) Providing Contact planes to call for flares at Zero plus 5 hours, Zero plus 6 hours and at 14.00 and 16.00 hours

(b) Patrolling the front by counter attack plane from Zero to dusk. In the event of a counter attack this plane will drop white parachute lights over the centre of the hostile troops.

7. ACKNOWLEDGE.

W.Pidsley.
Captain.
Brigade Major, 7th Infantry Brigade

Issued through signals at... Zero Hrs.

Copies to:-
1. 9th Devon Regt.
2. 20th Manchester Regt.
3. 21st Manchester Regt.
4. 7th L.T.M. Battery.
5. 74th Infantry Brigade
6. 75th Infantry Brigade
7. 25th Division "G"
8. Brigade Signal Officer
9. Staff Captain
10. War Diary.
11. File (2 Copies)

SECRET.   Copy No. 3

7TH INFANTRY BRIGADE INSTRUCTIONS NO 3.

SERIES "T"   3rd November 1918.

Ref. Map. 1/20000 Sheets 57A N.W. and 57B N.E.

1. Reference Instructions No. 2.

   (a) Moves for Y day will be carried out on 3rd November.

   (b) Amended times for passing starting points will be as follows:-

       21st Manchester Regt. (less 2 Coys)   15.50
       9th Devon Regt.   16.00
       20th Manchester Regt.   16.18

   (c) Trench Mortar Sections will march with their Battalions.

   (d) Brigade Headquarters will close at LE CATEAU and open at POMMEREUIL (near Advanced Division) at 16.00 hours.

2. Two companies of 21st Manchester Regt. came under orders of 75th Infantry Brigade at 09.00 hours today.

3. Four cyclist orderlies will be attached to 7th Infantry Brigade from Corps Cyclists from 12.00 hours today.

4. Reference Instructions No. 1. para 8 b 11 is cancelled.

5. Communications. Line of advance, as previously given extends along the LANDRECIES - MAROILLES road to 3.30.b.0.9. thence Le PRESEAU - LA PLANCHESSERIE - OLD MILL LES PRES (H.9.)
   Cable will cross canal N. of LANDRECIES and run N.E. of the Town.

6. Prisoners of War Cage will be at L.26.d.7.5. and will go forward with Division Headquarters in the event of its moving.

                                        W Paisley
                                        Captain.
ACKNOWLEDGE.   Brigade Major, 7th Infantry Brigade.

Issued through signals
at ....1300.... hours.

        Copies to:-
                1. 9th Devon Regt.
                2. 20th Manchester Regt.
                3. 21st Manchester Regt.
                4. 7th L.T.M. Battery.
                5. 74th Infantry Brigade.
                6. 75th Infantry Brigade.
                7. 25th Division "G"
                8. Bde Signal Officer.
                9. Staff Captain.
                10. War Diary.
                11. File.

SECRET.   Copy No. 4

7TH INFANTRY BRIGADE INSTRUCTIONS NO 3.

SERIES "T"   3rd November 1918.

Ref. Map. 1/20000 Sheets 57A N.W. and 57B N.E.

1. Reference Instructions No.2:-

    (a) Moves for Y day will be carried out on 3rd November.

    (b) Amended times for passing starting points will be as follows:-

        21st Manchester Regt (less 2 Coys)   15.50
        9th Devon Regt.   16.00
        20th Manchester Regt.   16.18

    (c) Trench Mortar Sections will march with their Battalions.

    (d) Brigade Headquarters will close at LE CATEAU and open at POMMEREUIL (near Advanced Division) at 16.00 hours.

2. Two companies of 21st Manchester Regt. came under orders of 75th Infantry Brigade at 09.00 hours today.

3. Four cyclist orderlies will be attached to 7th Infantry Brigade from Corps Cyclists from 12.00 hours today.

4. Reference Instructions No.1. para 8.6. will be cancelled.

5. Communications. Line of advance as previously given extends along the LANDRECIES - MARPILLES road to G.30.b.0.9. thence LE PRESEAU - LA BLANCHISSERIE - OLD MILL LES PRES (H.S.)
Cable will cross canal N. of LANDRECIES and run N.E. of the Town.

6. Prisoners of War Cage will be at L.26.d.7.8. and will go forward with Division Headquarters in the event of its moving.

ACKNOWLEDGE

                                        W. Pidsley.
                                        Captain,
Issued through signals   Brigade Major, 7th Infantry Brigade.
at....13.00.....hours.

Copies to:-
1. 9th Devon Regt.
2. 20th Manchester Regt.
3. 21st Manchester Regt.
4. 7th L.T.M. Battery.
5. 74th Infantry Brigade.
6. 75th Infantry Brigade.
7. 25th Division "G"
8. Bde Signal Officer.
9. Staff Captain.
10. War Diary.
11. File.

S E C R E T.   COPY NO. 21

75TH INFANTRY BRIGADE INSTRUCTIONS NO. 4 – SERIES "A".

Ref. map 1/40,000 Sheets 57A & 57B.   3/11/18.

1. **COMMUNICATIONS.**
   (a) Officer i/c Brigade Signals is arranging to have two lines laid from Brigade Headquarters in SALGARNI to all Battalion Headquarters by Z minus 6 hours.
   (b) In addition Officer i/c Brigade Signals is arranging to have dumped at Battalion Headquarters by Zero sufficient cable to lay a line to new Battalion Headquarters as they move forward as far as LANDRECIES.
   (c) Advance Brigade Report Centre will be established in the vicinity of G.16d.8.2. as soon as the Red Line has been gained.
   (d) Reference Instructions No. 1. Series A., the line of advance and trunk Line of communication forward of the Canal will run along the LANDRECIES – MAROILLES ROAD as far as G.30b.19 – thence to PRESEAU (H.19a.) – LA BLANCHISSERIE (H.13d) – OLD MILL DESPRES (H8b).
   Signal cable will cross the canal N. of LANDRECIES and will be laid on N.E. side of the Town.

2. **TANKS.** (2)
   The usual signals will be used between tank and Infantry.
   (a) *From Infantry to tank*

   Helmet waved on rifle – Tank wanted here.
   N.B. Rifle should be pointed in the direction of the obstruction.
   (b) *From tanks to Infantry.*
   (1) Red & Yellow Flag – Tank broken down; dont wait.
   (2) Green & White Flag – All's well, come on.
   (3) Tricolour Flag – British tank coming back to rally.

3. **PRISONERS OF WAR.**
   Prisoners of war will be escorted by Battalions to Bde. Hqrs. at L.18c.6.3. From here they will be sent on to Divisional Cage. Should Bde. Hd. Qrs. move the assembly point of prisoners will also be moved to a position close to the new Headquarters.

(4. **SMOKE.**
   Ref. Instr. No. 2, Series A., para 12.
   In addition to areas mentioned already, 15th Wing R.A.F. has arranged to place a smoke screen on spurs G.12d, H.7c.

5. **ROADS.**
   (a) The following roads are allotted to this Division for operations from noon "Y" day –
   1– LE CATEAU – POMMEREUIL – L.29a – L24 (IX Corps) also have running rights). This road will be allotted exclusively to 66th Division when the occasion arises.
   (2) LE CATEAU – L.20 – L.13 Road (allotted to 25th and 50th Division).

6. **ACTION OF /32ND DIVISION AFTER REACHING RED LINE.**
   96th Inf. Bde., 32nd Division, has received orders that after reaching Red Line it will be ready if sufficient daylight remains and 25th Division is ready to go forward, to conform to the movements of the 25th Division and occupy the high ground in Squares G.36, H.26 and H.21., so as to cover the Right Flank of the 25th Division.

7. **LIAISON POSTS.**
   Ref. Instr. No. 2, Series A. para 6. is cancelled.

OVER

Liaison Posts will be established as follows:-

Location of Posts.   Manned by

	Unit of 7th Bde.	Unit of 149th Bde.	Unit of 96th Bde.	Unit of 7th Bde.
G21b.3.0.	-------	---	15th. Lanc. Fus.	21st. Manch. Regt.
G22a.0.0.	1/5th Glos Regt.	---	-do-	-do-
G.22b.5.0.	1/8th Worc. Regt.	---	-do-	---
G.23c.0.2. (Practice Trenches)	1/8th Worc. Regt.	---	16th Lancs. Fus	---
G.16s.9.7.	1/8th R. War. Regt.	3rd R. Fus.	---	---
G.17b.7.0.	1/8th Worc. Regt.	-do-	---	---

6. ACKNOWLEDGE.

                                                                    [signature]
                                                                    Captain
Issued through Signals at   For Brigade Major, 75th Infantry Bde.
at *1200 hours*

Distribution as for Instructions No. 2, Series A.

Saddle Bag

21st (S) Battalion The Lancashire Regiment.

NARRATIVE of Events from 3rd to 4th NOV. 1918.

Ref: Map.- FRANCE 57 a. N.E. 1/20,000.

Date.	Hour.	Narrative.
3/11/18.	14.30 hrs.	A & C. Coys. left Station IX BATEAU and moved via TO...HILL to take over from left Company 15th Lancashire Fusiliers. Posts were taken over from C. 20. b. 5. 7. to C. 20. b. 30. 00. by 2 platoons of A. Company. C. Coy. and two remaining platoons of A. Company were formed up on tape from C. 20. a. 3.6. to C. 20. a. 80. 00. Relief complete by 19.30 hrs. Headquarters established at C. 20. a. 7. 8.
		TASK:-
		To mop area included in triangle C.20. a. 3. 6. - C. 20. a. 8. 0. - C. 23. a. 0. 0. and to establish liaison posts at C. 22. a. 0. 0. and C. 21. b. 4. 0. with 1/5th Gloucesters on our left and 15th Lancashire Fusiliers on right.
4/11/18.		Zero hour fixed for 06.15 hrs.
		Our advanced posts were withdrawn by 05.15 hrs. At 05.40 hrs. the Corps on Right (less the Coy. of the 15th Lancashire Fusiliers on our immediate right) advanced under a barrage. At 06.15 hrs. our barrage opened and we advanced under cover of it gaining all our objectives by 07.45. Posts were established but liaison with flanking units was not obtained until about 09.00 hrs. The 76th Brigade on our left advanced and captured LANDRECIES. A & C. Coys. then re-organised and at 15.30 hrs. again came under orders of our own Battalion Commander.
		During the advance we captured about 120 prisoners and many machine guns. We also liberated many civilians in HAPPEGARBES.
		Our casualties were 2 officers wounded (Second Lieut: F. SCHOFIELD and Second Lieutenant T. S. Bellis) 1 other rank killed and 12 other ranks wounded.
10/11/18.		*Chu Samuar* Lieutenant Colonel, Commanding 21st Bn. The Lancashire Regiment.

Casualties for the month of November, 1918.

3/11/18. Sec.Lieut.F.Schofield & Sec.Lieut.F.W.Bellis wounded.
7/11/18. Captain J.W.Bell M.C. killed in action.

Operations 3/7-11-18 Other Ranks. Killed 11, Wounded 63, Missing 3, D of W 1.

Reinforcements for the month of November, 1918.

1/11/18.	O.R's 105.
5/11/18.	" 30.
12/11/18.	Captain H.H.Field, 2Lieut.H.Henshall &
13/11/18.	Sec.Lieut.P.Sankey, M.M. and 51 O.R's.
15/11/18.	O.R. 1. Capt.R.G.Peel, T/Lieut.D.L.Townshend, Sec.Lieut.A.J. Wells.
17/11/18.	Lieut.H.E.Thornton, M.C.
22/11/18.	T/Major.H.W.Walker, M.C. & 5 O.R's.
26/11/18.	Sec.Lieut.H.H.Hilton, and 6 O.R's.
27/11/18.	Sec.Lieut.H.S.Price. and 9 O.R's.
30/11/18.	Sec.Lieuts.T.R.Trafford, R.Nicholas., G.Ingram., T.B.Hughes., H.Burke, M.M., T/Lieutenants.P.Shenton., L.A.Chadwick.

21st (S) Battalion The Manchester Regiment.

NARRATIVE of OPERATIONS from 3rd – 8th NOVEMBER, 1918.

Reference Map.- FRANCE Sheet 57 a. 1/40.000.

Date.	Hour.	NARRATIVE.
3/11/18.	09.00 hrs.	A & C. Coys. came under orders of 75th Infy. Bde.
	15.50 "	Battalion (less above) plus 1 section 7th T.M.B. and A. Echelon Regimental Transport left LE CATEAU for bivouacs in vicinity of POMMEREUIL, move completed 18.30 hrs. Bn.H.Q. at L. 27. c. 70. 80.
4/11/18.	05.45 hrs.	Zero for IX Corps.
	06.15 "	Zero for XIII Corps.
	12.00 "	Objective of 2 Companies reported gained at 07.45 hrs. with about 100 prisoners.
	14.15 hrs.	Battalion moved to vicinity of MALGARNI where A & C. Coys. were picked up. Battalion took up defensive position in reserve on S.W. side of LANDRECIES - ROBERSART Road.
	22.40 hrs.	Battalion disposed as follows:- Bn.H.Q. & R.A.P.- L. 21. b. 50. 80. A. Echelon.- L. 21. a. 60. 80. D. Coy. (L) & B. Coy. (R) along Railway Line from L. 16. d. 6. 4. to L. 22. a. 0. 2. A. Coy. Support.- vicinity of L. 21.b. 80. 40. C. Coy. Reserve.- vicinity of L. 21.b. 50. 50.
5/11/18.	10.30 hrs.	Battalion left assembly area. A. Echelon accompanied Battalion.- Route LANDRECIES-PRESEAU.
	12.00 hrs.	Reached Cattilon Farm thence to MAROILLES.
	14.20 hrs.	On arrival at MAROILLES Brigade Major ordered Battalion to go up to BASSE NOYELLE and to rejoin column of 7th Brigade at TAISNIERES.
	16.20 hrs.	Battalion reached BASSE NOYELLE. Several M.G.posts and snipers in vicinity of village.
6/11/18.	00.05 hrs.	Touch established with WILTS on Left - at I. 1. a. 3. 8. Companies in Line Right to Left:- A. Coy.- H. 11. d. 8. 6. - H. 12. a. 8. 8. D. " H. 12. a. 8. 8. - H. 6. d. 9. 7. B. " H. 6. d. 9. 7. - I. 1. a. 6. 7. In Reserve.- C. Coy about Rue-des-Haies. Bn.H.Q. at H. 6. c. 8. 6. Touch established with 9th Yorks at H. 11. d. 6. 8.
	10.35 hrs.	Battalion advanced as part of main body of 7th Infy. Bde.
	17.15 hrs.	Final dispositions:- Bn.H.Q. & R.A.P. opposite Church TAISNIERES. C. Coy.- LES CATTIAUX. D, B & A. Coys.- Billetted along main road of TAISNIERES. A. Echelon.- at about I. 2. d. 50. 45.
7/11/18.		Battalion ordered to act as Advanced Guard to 7th Infy. Bde. Boundaries.- Northern boundary line due E. from C.30.d. 5. 4. Southern boundary line due E. from I. 10; central objective E. 26. central to K. 7 central. 7th Brigade reported Outpost Line held by 20th Manchester Regiment as follows:- J. 7.central - J. 1. d. 4. 3. thence along Railway to N. boundary.

Date.	Hour.	Narrative.
7/11/18.	08.00 hrs.	Battalion disposed as follows:-

B. Coy. drawn up on Line J. 7. central to J. 1. d. 1. 4.
D. Coy. drawn up on Line I. 6. d. 5. 7. - O. 30. d. 5. 4.
A. Coy. in vicinity of I. 6. a. 5. 2.
C. Coy. and Bn.H.Q. along road with head of column at J. 7. a. 8. 9.
Advanced Report Centre.- J. 1. d. 1. 4.
There was a very thick mist which rendered the advance very difficult. It was found that the enemy had retired and cavalry patrols of 12th Lancers reported the following areas free of the enemy.-
J. 2. b. central - J. 8. b. central.
J. 4. central - wood J. 9. b. & J. 10. a.
nevertheless it was decided that on account of the fog the advance should be carried out as arranged.

09.45 hrs. Following line had been made good. No enemy encountered Road J. 3. b. 1. 9. - J. 3. c. 5. 6. - J. 9. a.0.0.

10.30 hrs. Major General Commanding Division came to J.1. d.1.4. and ordered advance to be carried out along AVESNES Road from J. 3. a. 3. 6. onwards. Battalion therefore

10.40 hrs. concentrated about J. 3. c. 5. 6. and advanced along road protected by scouts and 1 platoon C. Coy.
Order of Advance C.A.D.B. & H.Q.Coys. A. Echelon 1st Line Transport.

12.30 hrs. Patrols pushed out to CRAISETTE FARM to occupy farm.

12.50 hrs. Slight enemy resistance encountered at about J.10. d. 7. 5. Head of column J. 10. d. 2. 4. Bn.H.Q. on road J. 9. b. 8. 1.

13.00 hrs. 2 platoons extended to overcome resistance - advanced as far as line J. 10. b. 8. 2. - J. 11. c. 0. 4. Further resistance was encountered estimated machine guns were firing on our men. No touch on either flank at 13.00 hrs.

13.30 hrs. B. Coy. ordered to withdraw from column and proceed via J. 4. c. 1. 4. to establish posts at LACRAISETTE FARM - J. 4. b. 2. 7. - J. 5. a. 0. 8. - J. 5.b.2.8. and to establish touch with 50th Division on Left also to send one platoon to try and work round in rear of enemy machine guns which were holding up an advance and were situated on high ground in J. 11. central.

14.32 hrs. Vickers guns fired 5.000 rounds on to high ground in J. 11 central from positions at about J. 4. c. 7. 7.
C. Coy. attempted to advance again but were still held up.
The mist became very thick and it was impossible to locate the positions of the machine guns which were holding up the advance.

15.45 hrs. All above posts established and one platoon advancing South from J. 5. b. 1. 9. to-wards Pt.205. C. Coy still held up on Line J. 10. b. 8. 2. - J. 11.c.0.4.

14.00 hrs. Touch with 7th Brigade on Right established at
They were also held up by machine guns on sp in J. 11. central & J. 11. d.

16.30 hrs. Situation no change. Orders received that no adv should be carried out after this hour.

Date.	Hour.	NARRATIVE.
7/11/18.	18.00 hrs.	Following line had been taken up as Defensive Line for night 7/8th November:- D. Coy.- J. 10. a. 8. O.CRAISETTE FARM inclusive. B. Coy.- J. 5. c. 2. 1 with posts at J. 5. c. 3. 5. - J. 5 central - J. 5. b. 5. 1 J. 5. b. 1. 9. J. 5. a; 1. 9. J. 4. b. 2. 7. A. Coy.- vicinity of J. 3. d. central. C. " J. 3. c. central. Bn.H.Q. House at J. 3. c. 9. 4. No touch with 50th Division on Left. Battalion was relieved by 6th Inniskillings.Fusiliers.
8/11/18.	00.18 hrs.	Relief complete. Battalion proceeded to billets in DOMPIERRE.
	02.00 hrs.	All billeted.

Strength on going into line 5/11/18.   Officers   Other Ranks.
                                           15   544

Chudanax Lieutenant Colonel,
Commanding 21st Bn. The Manchester Regiment.

	Killed.	Wounded.	Missing.	D. of W.	Sick.
Officers.	1	2	-	-	-
Other Ranks.	11	64	4	-	6
Prisoners (estimated).		150			

SECRET.   Copy No.........

7TH INFANTRY BRIGADE ORDER NO.24.

Ref. Map. 57A.1/40000.   5th November 1918.

1. The outpost line tonight is held by the 74th Inf. Brigade on the Right from approximately H.17.b.9.5, H.11.d.5.9., H.11.b.4.1., H.5.c.0.0. and on the Left by 7th Inf. Bde. (21st Manchester Regt) from H.5.c.0.0. along road to BASSE NOYELLES. (H.Q. at H.5.b.6.1.)
The 21st Manchester Regt. and 9th Devon Regt. are dug in along the road H.10.c. and H.16.b. with Headquarters H.10.c.4.4.

2. The advance will be continued on the 6th November on a Two Brigade Front., 74th Infantry Brigade on the Right and 7th Inf. Brigade on Left.

3. The 7th Inf. Brigade Southern Boundary Line due EAST from H.12.central to J.7.central (the stream in I.10. inclusive to 7th Inf. Bde.) Northern Boundary Line due EAST through C.26.c. 0.5.

4. Line of advance MAROILLES, Cross Roads H.11.c.4.4. - BASSE NOYELLES - I.3.a.0.7. - Road junction I.2.d.9.3. - I.3.b.5.1. - I.12.central.

5. Objective line from cross roads J.7.b.2.0. to cross roads J.2.a.2.5. (both inclusive).

6. Advance Guard to 7th Infantry Brigade will be composed of :-

Advance Guard Commander.   Lieut. Col. C.R.Pilkington.C.M.G.
20th Manchester Regt.
One Troop of 12th Lancers.   (less one section)
One section 105. Field Coy. R.E.

will advance so as to pass the outpost line at RUE DES HAIES (H.6.c.0.0.) at 06.30 hours, with a view to making good the Final Objective. O.C. Advance Guard will endeavour to push on and save from destruction the Bridge at I.3.a.8.0. using the cavalry and R.E's allotted to him to the best possible advantage.

7. Order of March of Main Body.

9th Devon Regt.
21st Manchester Regt.
Coy. 23th M.G.Battalion.
105. Field Coy. R.E.
150th Bde. R.F.A.

50 yards will be maintained between Platoons and 300 yards between Units. O.C. 9th Devon Regt. will regulate his distance from the Advance Guard according to the nature of the country. This should not be greater than one mile, and Head of his column should be at the square MAROILLES H.16.b. at 06.30 hours

8. Brigade Headquarters will remain at G.15.d.5.5. moving subsequently along the line of advance.

                                                W.Pilsley.

9. ACKNOWLEDGE.
                                                Captain.
                                        Brigade Major, 7th Infantry Brigade.

Issued through signals
at 19.30 hours.

SPECIAL ORDER.

I wish to call to the notice of all ranks the names of the undermentioned N.C.Os. and men who performed exceptionally fine work during the recent operations and to place on record my appreciation of the splendid services which they rendered:-

H.Q. Coy.
203116 Pte. Russell J.
64176 Pte. Holding P.
34016 Pte. Pack E.
45461 L/C. Boardman P.

A. Coy.
... L/C. Hughes A.
... Pte. ...
60... Pte. Witherns H.
58034 Pte. Baldwin J.S.

B. Coy.
...... A/Cpl. Lester P.
51.... Pte. Penterton P.
30... Pte. Hall A.
61456 Pte. Dewhurst J.

C. Coy.
36180 Pte. Ogden A.
30... " Campion E.
..... " Sneddon J.
41... " Ehlers E.

D. Coy.
...... L/C. Eastwood J.
12... Sgt. Mixinson D.
41865 L/C. Roberts W.
..... Pte. Turnbull J.

Signed,
Lieutenant Colonel,
Commanding 21st Bn. The Lancs. Fusiliers.

11/11/18.

SECRET/ 21st Bn. The Manchester Regiment.

Operation Order No.161.

Ref.Map 57b 1/40.000.   13th November, 1918.
                    to-day
1. Battalion will move to xxxxxxx to POMMEREUIL.
   Time.- 11.00 hrs.
   Starting Point:- Square,C.25.a.7.4. (near FACTORY) facing WEST.
   DRESS.- Full marching order.
   ROUTE.- HAPPEGARBES - C. 20. c. 6. 1. - L. 29. a. 4. 3.
   Order of march.- H.Q. BAND, A.B.C.D.Coys. Regtl.Transport.

2. One lorry has been allotted to the Brigade for transport of blankets,
   it will make two journeys, 2nd journey for half blankets of 20th
   Manchesters and the whole of the blankets of the 21st Manchesters.
   It should report here at approximately 10.30 hrs.

3. All officers valises and mess boxes and blankets(rolled in bundles
   of ten) will be stacked outside Q.Ms. Stores by 10.00 hrs. Packs of
   the band will be dumped along with blankets and one man detailed to
   remain with them. They will be carried, if possible with the blankets
   if not, our own transport will return for them and such extra stores
   as may be left behind.

4. Billeting parties with bicycles will report to Second Lieutenant
   G.R.BIRCH,M.L. at Bn.Orderly Room at 09.00 hrs. This party will
   report to Staff Captain at POMMEREUIL at 10.00 hrs.

5. Baggage guard of 1 platoon (B.Coy to report to P.O.10.00 hrs.under an
6. ACKNOWLEDGE.   officer.
   Issued at 08.00 hrs.ByRunner.   Lieutenant & A/Adjt,
                                               21st Bn. The Manchester Regt.

To all concerned.

Secret.   21st Bn., The Manchester Regiment.   Copy No. 13
Operation Order No. 162

Reference Map :- Valenciennes 1/100,000.   28th November, 1918.

1. Battalion will move to QUIEVY to-morrow, 29th November.

2. Detail as follows:-
   Starting Point:- Pommereuil Church facing North.
   Route:- Road Junction 3/4 mile W of P in Pommereuil - Montay - Neuvilly
   Station - Briastre-Farm, 1 1/4 miles E of Quievy.
   Time :- 0920 hours.
   Order of march:- Headquarters, A, B, C & D Coys, Regimental Transport.
   Dress:- Full marching Order. Caps will be worn.
   Intervals:- 100 yds between Companies and 50 yards between every 12 vehicles.

3. Baggage Arrangements.
   (a) All blankets will be rolled as for Pack Transport Transport and stacked at Q.M.Stores by 0700 hours.
   (b) All Orderly Room Baggage, Q.M.Stores and Cooks utensils will be dumped at Q.M.Stores by 0700 hours.
   (c) All Officers Valises, Mess Boxes etc will be stacked at Bn.Orderly Room by 0800 hours.

4. O.C. "A" Coy will detail 1 Platoon under an officer to report to T.O. at 0715 hours at Q.M.Stores to act as leading party and Baggage Party.

5. Dinners will be served on arrival at new area.

6. Billetting Party under 2Lieut. Birch will assemble at Church at 0645 hours and subsequently report to 2Lieut. Liddiard at Church QUIEVY at 0900 hours

7. Os.C.Coys will report Coys correctly billetted as soon as possible Codeword - FARNDON.

8. Acknowledge.

Issued by Runner at 2130 hours.   T. Orgill
                                          Captain & Adjutant.
                                          21st Battalion The Manchester Regiment.

Usual distribution.

After Order.
                                                         28th November, 1918.
1. DETAIL.
   Para. 2 of R.Os of to-night is cancelled and the following is substituted:-

   Reveille   0600 hours.
   B'fast.   0715   "
   Sick Parade. 0715   "
   Orderly Room. 1615   "

                                (sd) E.F. Orgill Captain & Adjutant.
                                21st Battalion The Manchester Regiment.

SECRET.   Copy No......3...

7TH INFANTRY BRIGADE ORDER NO.27.

Ref. Map. VALENCIENNES   28th November 1918.
1/100000.

1.   The 7th Infantry Brigade Group (less D.A.C. and 106th Field Coy. R.E.) will march to QUIEVY on 29th November in accordance with Table overleaf.

2.   Distances will be maintained as laid down in G.R.O.5588 of 18th November; i.e. 500 yards between Battalions, 100 yards between Companies and 50 yards between every 12 vehicles.

3.   (a)   Billetting Parties report to Battalion Forward Representative at CHURCH, QUIEVY at 09.00 hours.

        (b)   Billetting Certificates for this village to be rendered and certificates obtained from Area Commandant that billets are left clean.

4.   (a)   Transport will march in rear of Units.

        (b)   Motor Transport - one lorry will report to each Infantry Battalion at 07.00 hours and do two journeys. One lorry for 77th Field Ambulance and Brigade Headquarters will report at Brigade H.Q. at 07.00 hours

5.   Brigade Headquarters will close at POMMEREUIL at 10.30 hours and open at S. end of QUIEVY on arrival.

6.   ACKNOWLEDGE. (Bde. Group only.)

                                            W Pidsley.
                                                        Captain.
Issued through signals   Brigade Major, 7th Infantry Brigade.
at:-......1130.hours.

Copies to:-   1. 9th Bn. Devon Regt.
               2. 20th Bn. Manchester Regt.
               3. 21st Bn. Manchester Regt.
               4. 7th L.T.M.Battery.
               5. Bde. Signal Officer.
               6. 77th Field Ambulance.
               7. 11th Bn. South Lancs Regt.
               8. 106th Field Coy. R.E.
               9. 25th D.A.C.
              10. Staff Captain.
              11. Bde. Transport Officer.
              12. 25th Division "Q"
              13. A.P.M.
              14. War Diary.
              15. File.
              16. Area Commandant POMMEREUIL.

MARCH TABLE.

UNIT.	To pass Starting Point. Brigade Headquarters.	Route.	Remarks.
7th Inf. Bde. H.Q. and 7th T.M.Battery.	09.10.	Road Junction ¾ mile W. of P. in POMMEREUIL. - MONTAY - NEUVILLY STATION - BRIASTRE - FARM 1½ miles EAST OF QUIEVY.	Usual halts. Dinners on arrival.
20th Manchester Regt.	09.14.	do.	do.
21st Manchester Regt.	09.30.	do.	do.
9th Bn. Devon Regt.	09.45.	do.	do.
77th Field Ambulance	10.10.	do.	do.
11th Bn. South Lancs. Regt.	10.15.	do.	do.

WAR DIARY.
for Month of December 1918.

CONTENTS.

1. War Diary.

APPENDICES.

Appendix. 1. 7th Infantry Brigade Order.
Appendix. 2. Battalion Order.

1st January, 1918.

[signature] Major,
Commanding 21st Battalion Manchester Regiment.

WAR DIARY
or
INTELLIGENCE SUMMARY.

Army Form C.

Volume 58.
December, 1918.

21st Bn. The Manchester Regiment.

Place	Date	Hour	Summary of Events and Information	Remarks references to Appendices
BUIRE.	1.		In Billets. Fine.	
	2.		do. Training and Salvage.	
	3.		do. do.	
	4.		do. do.	
	5.		do. do.	
	6.		do. do.	
	7.		do. do.	
	8.		do. do.	
	9.		do. Fair.	
	10.		do. Showery.	
	11.		do. Fair.	
	12.		do. do.	
	13.		do. Fine.	
	14.		do. do.	
	15.		do. do.	
	16.		do. do.	
	17.		do. do.	
	18.		do. do.	
	19.		do. do.	
	20.		do. Fair.	
	21.		do. do.	
	22.		do. do.	
	23.		do. do.	
	24.		do. do.	
	25.		Christmas Day. Fair.	
	26.		do. Fair.	
	27.		do. Training and Salvage work. Fair.	
	28.		The Battalion left BUIRE for BARASTCOURT at 1030 hrs. In Billets 1230 hrs. As King's visit.	
BARASTCOURT.	29.		In Billets. Fine. Parades and Salvage Work. (Fair)	
	30.		do. Fair.	
	31.		do. do.	

List of Officers and Casualties attached.

B. Mullman Major.
COMMANDING 21st BN. THE MANCHESTER REGIMENT.

Reinforcements for the Month of December 1918.

```
5/12/18.        Sec:Lieut. P.C.Tomlinson,  and 47 Other Ranks.
9/12/18.        4 Other Ranks.
12/12/18.       8      do
13/12/18.       5      do
17/12/18.       1      do
24/12/18.       1      do
23/12/18.       Lie. [?]eut. J. Fletcher.
```

Casualties for the Month of December 1918.

NIL.

7th Infantry Brigade No. S.764/400/19.

21st Manchester Regt.
Area Commandant, BETHENCOURT.
201st Coy. R.A.S.C.
25th Division."G"

1. The 21st Manchester Regt. will march to BETHENCOURT on 28th December and go into billets to be obtained direct from the Area Commandant.

2. Usual distances will be maintained - Route and time are left to the discretion of O.C. 21st Manchester Regt.

3. Arrival in billets will be reported to Brigade Headquarters.

24/12/18.
Captain.
Brigade Major, 7th Infantry Brigade.

SECRET 21st Bn. The Manchester Regiment. Copy No. 9
OPERATION ORDER No.163
                     27th DECEMBER, 1918.

1. The Battalion will move to BETHENCOURT to-morrow 28th instant.

2. Starting Point.- Parish Church.
   Time.- 1030 hrs.
   Order of March.- Band, H.Q. B.C.D.A.Coys. Regimental Transport.
   Usual distances will be maintained.

3. Billeting arrangements as already detailed.

4. Baggage arrangements.
   (a) Blankets will be rolled as for pack transport and stacked in transport yard by 0900 hrs.
   (b) Transport Officer will detailed:-
      1. 2 limbers to report to each Company Mess and 1 limber to H.Q. Mess at 0930 hrs. for the conveyance of Officers' kit and mess gear.
      2. 1 limber to be at the disposal of the Adjutant for moving Orderly Room boxes at any time it is required.

5. ACKNOWLEDGE.
                 Captain & Adjutant,
            21st Battalion The Manchester Regiment.

1. C.O. 2. O.C.A.Coy. 3. O.C.B.Coy. 4. O.C. C.Coy. 5. O.C.D.Coy.
6. O.C.H.Q.Coy. 7. Transport Officer. 8. Adjutant. 9. & 10. War Diary.
11. File.

21st (S) Battalion The Manchester Regiment.
WARNING ORDER.

app 2

The Battalion will move to BETHENCOURT on the 28th inst.
Billeting arrangements are as follows:-
C.Q.M.Sgts and an N.C.O. from Transport will meet the Adjutant at the Area Commandants Office (near the Church) Bethencourt at 1015 hrs tomorrow
It is suggested that Companies each send over a party to clean up billets and Messes - they could take rations and spend the night there.

Acknowledge.

Issued at
By runner

26th December, 1918.

F. Y Gill
Captain,
Adjutant 21st Battalion The Manchester Regiment.

WAR DIARY.

for

Month of January. 1919.

CONTENTS.

I.   War Diary.

APPENDICES.

Appendix: I.   Battalion Operations Orders.

Appendix. 2.   Warning Orders.

2nd February 1919.   *Gustavar*   Lieut-Colonel.
                          Commanding 21st Bn; The Manchester Regiment.

Army Form C. 2118.

WAR DIARY
or
INTELLIGENCE SUMMARY.

21st Battalion The Manchester Regiment. January 1919. Volume 39

Place	Date	Hour	Summary of Events and Information	Remarks and references to Appendices
BETHENCOURT	1.		In Billets. Training and Salvage work. Fair.	
do	2.		do do	
POIX DU NORD	3.		The Bn. left BETHENCOURT at 1030 hours and proceeded by March Route to POIX DU NORD. All in billets by 1600 hours. Fine.	
do	4.		In Billets. Training and Salvage work. Fine. "B" Company moved into billets at VENDEGIES.	
do	5.		In Billets. Training and Salvage work. Fair.	
do	6.		do do Wet.	
do	7.		do do Fair.	
do	8.		do do do	
do	9.		do do do	
do	10.		do do do	
do	11.		do do do	
do	12.		do do do	
do	13.		do do do	
do	14.		do do do	
do	15.		do do Wet.	
do	16.		do do Fair.	
do	17.		do do do	
do	18.		do do do	
do	19.		do do do	
do	20.		do do do	
do	21.		do do do	
do	22.		do do do	
do	23.		do do do B Coy moved from VENDEGIES to Poix du Nord.	
do	24.		do do Frosty.	
do	25.		do do Snowing.	
do	26.		do do Frosty.	
do	27.		do do do	
do	28.		do do	

Army Form C. 2118.

WAR DIARY
or
INTELLIGENCE SUMMARY.
(Erase heading not required.)

21st Battalion The Manchester Regiment

Instructions regarding War Diaries and Intelligence Summaries are contained in F.S. Regs., Part II and the Staff Manual respectively. Title pages will be prepared in manuscript.

Place	Date	Hour	Summary of Events and Information	Remarks and references to Appendices
PUIX DU NORD	29		In Billets. Training and Salvage work. Frosty. Transport complete.	(1)
do	30		do do do	(2)
do	31.		do do Snowing.	(3)
			List of Reinforcements and Casualties attached.	

Cridaux Lieutenant Colonel;

Commanding 21st Battalion The Manchester Regiment

21st Bn. The MANCHESTER Regiment.

WARNING ORDER No.2.

1st January, 1919.

1. Reference para 5 of Warning Order issued to-day.
1 lorry will remark leave Bn. H.Q. at 1430 to-morrow with a load of unissued blankets etc. Owing to the lateness of the hour at which the lorry will start it will not be possible for the advance party to ride on same. They may, however, leave their packs and haversacks at the Q.M's Stores in charge of one man to be detailed by A. Coy. This man will see that the packs are put on the lorry and delivered to the rightful owners at BOIX DU NORD.
Billeting party will have to proceed by jumping lorries and motoring.

Acknowledge

J O'M
Captain & Adjutant,
21st Bn. The Manchester Regiment.

Usual distribution.

21st Bn. The MANCHESTER Regiment.

WARNING ORDER.

1st January, 1919.

1. The Battalion will move to POISE DE NORD on January 3rd.

2. Advance parties as under will parade at Bn. Orderly Room at 0845 hrs. to- the 2nd instant, and proceed under Second Lieutenant F.SANKEY,M.M. to POISE DE NORD where they will report to the Assistant Adjutant at the Church:-
   C.Q.M.S.'s.
   1 N.C.O. & 3 men per Coy.
   1 representative from transport and each section of H.Q.Coy.

3. It is possible that one or more lorries may be taking over surplus stores to-morrow - if this is so arrangements will be made to carry the equipment at least of the Advance Party.

4. ACKNOWLEDGE.

Captain & Adjutant,
21st Bn. The Manchester Regiment.

1. C.O. 2. Adjutant. 3. O.C.A.Coy. 4. O.C.B.Coy. 5. O.C.C.Coy.
6. O.C.D.Coy. 7. O.C.H.Q.Coy. 8. T.O. 9. Q.M. 10. R.S.M. 11. War Diary.
12. War Diary. 13. File.

SECRET/   21st Bn. The MANCHESTER Regiment.   Copy No. 15

OPERATION ORDER No.164.

Ref:Maps:- FRANCE SHEET   January 3rd 1919.
          1/40,000.

1. The Battalion will move to billets in POIX DU NORD on FRIDAY

2. DETAIL FOR MARCH.
   (a) Starting Point:- Road junction 60 yds. E. of B. Coy's Mess, facing EAST.
   (b) Time.- 1015 hrs.
   (c) ORDER OF MARCH.- Band, H.Q. - C.D.A.B.Coys. Regtl. transport.
   (d) Route.- INCHY - NEUVILLY - Road junctions at K.10.b.1.7. - K. 4. b. 1. - E. 29. a. 2. 3. - OVILLERS - VENDEGIES AU BOIS - Road junctions at F. 8. a. O. 1. - X 26 d. 1. 1. (sheets 51 A) - POIX DU NORD.
   (e) Distance.- 12 1/2 miles.
   (f) Usual distances to be maintained.
   (g) A halt during which tea will be issued will be observed from 1250 hrs to 1320 hrs.
   (h) DRESS.- Full marching order - steel helmets on back of packs.

3. BILLETTING ARRANGEMENTS.
   As already detailed in W.O. and W.O. 2 dated 1st January, 1919.

4. BAGGAGE ARRANGEMENTS.
   (a) Blankets rolled as for pack transport; officers kits and packs of band will be stacked in H.Q.Mess Yard at 0830 hrs. One man per Coy. will be detailed to guard and accompany blankets.
   (b) All mess kit above two boxes per Company will be stored in Q.M's Stores by 0900 hrs. as it will probably be impossible to move this kit until the 5th instant at the earliest. O.C. B. Coy. will detail one LanceCorporal and 3 other ranks to report to Quartermaster at 0900 hrs. to guard the above and any other surplus kit. Quartermaster will arrange to provide the guard with at least 3 days rations.
   (c) The Mess Cart will call at Company Officers' Messes between 0900 and 0945 hrs. to collect and carry two mess boxes only per Company.
   (d) Transport Officer will arrange to place a limber at the disposal of the Adjutant for moving Orderly Room kit.

5. Certificates that billets have been left scrupulously clean will be sent to Orderly Room by 1000 hrs. on 3rd instant.

6. O.C.Companies will report immediately all ranks are present in billets at POIX DU NORD stating the number that fell out on the line of march.

7. ACKNOWLEDGE.

Issued at   BY RUNNER.   Captain & Adjutant,
                                              21st Bn. The Manchester Regiment.

No. 1. C.O.   8. A/Adjutant.   15. War Diary.
    2. A. Coy.   9. T.O.   16. File.
    3. B. "   10. M.O.
    4. C. "   11. R.S.M.
    5. D. "   12. R.Q.M.S.
    6. HQ "   13. 7th Inf. Bde.
    7. Adjutant.   14. W.Diary.

Reinforcements for the Month of January 1919.

7.1.19.   4.Other Ranks.
18.1.19.   1. Other Rank.

Casualties for the Month of January 1919.

NIL.

WAR DIARY.
FOR
MONTH OF JANUARY, 1919.

CONTENTS.

I.   WAR DIARY.

APPENDICES.

Appendix. 1.   Brigade Operations Orders.
Appendix. 2.   Warning Orders.

C.O. 1/9.   *[signature]*   Lieut-Colonel.
                          Commanding 1/9. Battalion The Manchester Regt.

Army Form C. 2118.

WAR DIARY
or
INTELLIGENCE SUMMARY.
Volume 40.

21st Battalion The Manchester Regiment. February 1919.

Instructions regarding War Diaries and Intelligence Summaries are contained in F. S. Regs., Part II. and the Staff Manual respectively. Title pages will be prepared in manuscript.

Place	Date	Hour	Summary of Events and Information	Remarks and references to Appendices
POIX DU NORD.	1.		In Billets. Training and Salvage Work. Frosty.	
do	2.		do do do	
do	3.		do do do	
do	4.		do do do	
do	5.		do do do	
do	6.		do do do	
do	7.		do do do	
do	8.		do do do	
do	9.		do do do	
do	10.		do do do	
do	11.		do do do	
do	12.		do do Fine.	
do	13.		do do do	
do	14.		do do do	
do	15.		do do do	
do	16.		do do Raining.	
do	17.		do do Fair.	
do	18.		do do do	
do	19.		The Bn. left POIX DU NORD. at 0830 hours and proceeded by March Route to SOLESMES. all in Billets by 1200 hours. Fine.	
SOLESMES.	20.		The Bn. left SOLESMES. at 0830 hours and proceeded by March Route to CAMBRAI. all in Billets by 1430 hours. Fine.	
CAMBRAI.	21.		In Billets. Training and Salvage Work. Raining.	
do	22.		do do Showery.	
do	23.		do do Fair.	
do	24.		do do do	
do	25.		do do do	
do	26.		do do Showery.	
do	27.		do do do	
do	28.		do do do	

Andrews Lieut-Colonel.
Commanding 21st Battalion The Manchester Regt.

Reinforcements for the month of February 1919.

NIL.

Casualties for the Month of February 1919.

NIL.

7th Infantry Brigade No.B.M.431.

9th Devon Regt.
20th Manchester Regt.
21st Manchester Regt.
77th Field Ambulance.
106th Field Coy R.E.
7th L.T.M.Bty.

WARNING ORDER.

1. The 25th Division is concentrating in and around CAMBRAI, moves being carried out between the 17th and 22nd February.

2. The 7th Infantry Brigade Group less D.A.C. and 11th S.Lancs Regt will be billetted in CAMBRAI: other Units in the town being
   H.Q. 65th A.F.A. Brigade.
   266 Bty. A.F.A.
   505 "   "
   75th Infantry Brigade.
   25th Bn. M.G.Corps.

3. The Brigade will move by march route, staging one night at SOLESMES.

4. Competent Billetting parties under an Officer will be told off and prepared to go on in advance to both places early on the 17th February to make the best of the available accommodation.
   Billetting Strengths in Officers, Other Ranks and Horses to be rendered by 1800 hours, 16th February, together with a Return giving tonnage which cannot be moved by Regimental Transport.

4. Further orders will be issued as soon as received.

Captain,
15/2/19.   Brigade Major 7th Infantry Brigade.

7th Infantry Brigade No.B.M.434.
****

To - All recipients of Bde.Order No.31.
****

       Reference March Table attached to Bde.Order 31 of todays date.

       Serial No.6. - No.4.Coy R.A.S.C. will march to CAMBRAI on the 18th February and not on the 20th.

16/2/19.

                                              Captain,
                       Brigade Major 7th Infantry Brigade.

SECRET.   Copy No. 3

7th INFANTRY BRIGADE ORDER No.31.

Ref.Map : VALENCIENNES
         1/100.000.   16th February,1919.

1. The 7th Infantry Brigade Group will move by march route to CAMBRAI in accordance with attached table.

2. The usual distances will be maintained on the march and the usual halts observed.

3.(a) Billetting parties will proceed to destination so as to reach there at least 48 hours before the arrival of their Units. Parties for CAMBRAI can be accommodated at Divisional Reception Camp if notification of numbers is wired direct to the O.C.Camp.
   (b) Billets must be left clean.

4. All Stores and equipment will be taken - any which cannot be moved in the first instance will be left in charge of a Guard. This should include the gear which is the least essential to the comfort of the Troops.

5. Transport arrangements are as follows :-
   (a) The usual Regimental Transport and Baggage Wagons.
   (b) A certain number (to be notified later.) of extra G.S.Wagons.
   (c) A very limited number of lorries for one day, to be used to take Kit etc., through to CAMBRAI.
Numbers, times, and other administrative arrangements will be notified later.

6. Completion of all Moves to be notified to Bde Hd.Qrs.

7. Bde. H.Q. will close at POIX DU NORD at 0800 hours on 20th February and open at CAMBRAI on arrival.

8. ACKNOWLEDGE.

                                W. Pidsley
                                     Captain,
                         Brigade Major 7th Infantry Brigade.

Issued through
Signals at ....hours.

        Copies to :-
            1. 9th Devon Regt.   14. G.O.C.
            2. 20th Manchester Regt.   15. Brigade Major.
            3. 21st Lancaster Regt.   16. Staff Captain.
            4. 106 Field Coy R.E.   17. O.C.Signals.
            5. No.4.Coy Train.   18. War Diary.
            6. 7th L.T.M.Bty.   19. File.
            7. 77th Field Amb.
            8. 11th S.Lancs Regt.
            9. 25th Division.
           10. "   "
           11. Town Comdt.CAMBRAI.
           12. Town Major, SOLESMES.
           13. S.S.O., 25th Divn.

MARCH TABLE.

Date. 1919.	Serial No.	Unit.	From.	To.	Starting Point.	Time.	Route.	Billets from.	Remarks.
19th Feby.	1.	20th Manchesters	POIX DU NORD.	St.VAAST.	LA FILATURE (Westernmost house in POIX DU NORD.	0900 hours.	VENDEGIES. BEAURAIN. SOLESMES.		
"	2.	21st Manchesters.	POIX DU NORD.	St.PYTHON.	"	0910 hours.	do.	25th Bn. H.G.Corps.	Dismounted personnel of Bde.H.Q. & T.M.B.attached
"	3.	106 Fld.Co.R.E.	POIX DU NORD.	SOLESMES.	"	0920 hours.	do.	Town Major.	
"	4.	9th Devon Regt.	ENGLE-FONTAINE.	SOLESMES.	"	0930 hours.	do.	11.S.Lancs.	
20th Feby.	5.	7th Bde.H.Q. & T.M.Bty.	POIX DU NORD.	CAMBRAI.	Bde.H.Q.	0800 hours.	SOLESMES. St.VAAST. CAMBRAI.	Town Comdt. CAMBRAI	Dismounted personnel wit 21st Manch.or 19th Feby.
"	6.	No.4.Coy R.A.S.C.	SALESCHES.	CAMBRAI.	SALESCHES.	Any.	do.	do.	Time to be chosen by O.C Coy & Bde.H.Q notified.
"	7.	20th Manchesters.	ST.VAAST.	do.	St.VAAST Church.	1000 hours.	do.	do.	
"	8.	21st Manchesters.	ST.PYTHON.	do.	do.	1010 hours.	do.	do.	Halting East the village 0950 hours.
"	9.	9th Devons.	SOLESMES.	do.	do.	1020 hours.	do.	do.	
"	10.	106 Fld.Co.R.E.	do.	do.	do.	1030 hours.	do.	do.	

11th S.Lancs Regt. are moving from SOLESMES by 1000 hours on 18th Feby. under orders of 25th Division.

ADMINISTRATIVE INSTRUCTIONS
IN CONNECTION WITH 7th BRIGADE ORDER NO.31.

17th February 1919.

1. BILLETS. Billeting parties for Cambrai must proceed without fail by the mid-day train on 18th February, and report to Town Commandant Cambrai, immediately on arrival. Billeting will take some time and require good men with a knowledge of French if possible.
Billets require many repairs and any oiled linen available should be carried.
The Town Commandant's Office is situated on the S.W. outskirts of the town, just East of the Canal.

2. Transport will be alloted as follows:-

	G.S.Wagons.	3 Ton Lorries.
9th Devon Regt.	3	1
20th Manchester Regt.	3	1
21st Manchester Regt.	3	1
106 Field Company.	--	1
7th Bde. H.Q. T.M.B. & Cinema.	--	2

The G.S. Wagons for blankets etc., will report at Battalions H.Q. at 09.30 hours on 18th February, with 3 days rations, they will move with Battalions and be ordered to return to the D.A.C. on the morning of the 21st February.
Lorries will report at Battalions H.Q. at 09.00 hours on the 19th February, and should be ordered to do 2 complete through journeys to Cambrai on the 19th, they are not available for the 20th Feby., rendezvous with billeting parties in Cambrai must be arranged.

3. Brigade Headquarters will open at 08.00 hours on 20th February, at No.18, RUE DE LA PORTE ROBERT, (100 yards S. of the Officers Club.)

A report centre will be at above address from 08.00 hours 18th February. *under Lt Cromie M.C*

Supply arrangements later

Copies sent to:-

9th Devon Regt.   106 Field Company.
20th Manchester Regt.   7th Light T.M. Battery.
21st Manchester Regt.   201 Coy. R.A.S.C.

Captain.
Brigade Major 7th Infantry Brigade.

TRANSPORT TABLE.

Serial No.	Vehicle.	Allotted to.	On.	For conveyance of	Remarks.
A.	1 G.S.W.	A.Coy	19th & 20th.	Blankets, valises & mess tin.	Waggons to report today & remain with Coys until move on 20th is completed. Horses to report on 19th [illegible] 45 minutes before Bn. leaves the starting point.
B.	do	B.Coy	do	do	
C.	do	C.Coy	do	do	
D.	do	D.Coy.	do	do	
E.	do	Cookh.	do	Cooks stores etc.	
F.	[illegible]	[illegible]	do	Canteen, messings, stores.	Arrangements as to time of waggons reporting to be arranged between those concerned. Waggons to be ready to move 45 minutes before Bn. moves.
G.	1 Limber.	[illegible]	do	do do do	
H.	1 Limber.	H.Q. Coy.	do	Blankets.	
J.	1 Limber	Adjutant.	do	Office boxes and stores.	As for A.B.C.D.
K.	2 Limbers.	Bn. [illegible]	do	All Lewis Gun stores.	To be loaded today & return to Transport Lines.
L.	2 Limbers.	Transport.	do		
M.	1 Limber.	Cook Sgt.	19th.	Food.	
N.	1 [illegible]	[illegible]	19th & 20th.	[illegible] Kit & Valises.	Report at [illegible] minutes before Battalion moves.
O.	1-ton Lorry.	[illegible]	19th.	Stores.	Reports at 0800 hours. [illegible] Journeys direct to [illegible].

ADMINISTRATIVE INSTRUCTIONS TO ACCOMPANY O.O. NO. 16.

1. Transport will be allotted in accordance with attached table. All concerned must make sure that Transport is ready to move with the Battalion.

2. A baggage guard of 1 officer and 20 men will be provided by O.C. "B" Coy. They will report at B.H.Q. Stores at 0715 hours and load the vehicles allotted to them and march in rear of the transport.

3. AMMUNITION.

E H Gill
Captain & Adjutant,
1st Battalion The Manchester Regt.

Copies to all recipients
of Operation Order No. 16.

UNIT: 2nd Battalion The Manchester Regiment.   Ser. No. 12

MARCHING ORDER No. 14.

Ref: Map :- VALENCIENNES,   18th February 1919.
1:100,000

1. Battalion will move to billets in BELGIUM on 19th, 20th and 20th February 1919. The move will be carried out in two stages.

   (a) on 19th inst to ST. GHISLAIN.
   (b) on 20th inst to CHIMAY.

2. The following detail will be observed on 19th inst:-

   (a) Dress:- Full marching order—caps will be worn.
   (b) Order of march :- A, B, Colour Party, C, D Companies. Regtl Transport.
   (c) Usual halts and distances will be observed on the march.
   (d) Starting point:- Battalion HQ road, facing WEST.
   (e) Time :- 0845 hours.
   (f) Distance :- 8 miles.
   (g) Route :- VALENCIENNES, QUARAGNON, ST.GHISLAIN.

3. Details for move on 20th inst will be detailed verbally on 19th inst.

4. Administrative and baggage arrangements will be notified separately.

5. Usual certificates on vacating and on occupying billets will be rendered by O.C. Companies.

6. ACKNOWLEDGE.

Issued at   by Dispr.   E H Orjell
                                         Captain & Adjutant,
                                         2nd Battalion The Manchester Regiment.

No. 1. C.O.   7. ....
    2. Adjt.   8. ....
    3. A.Coy.   9. ....
    4. B.Coy.   10. Lewis M.G. Off.
    5. C.Coy.   11. The Euty Off.
    6. D.Coy.   12. I.O.
               13. War Diary.

Army Form C. 2118.

WAR DIARY
or
INTELLIGENCE SUMMARY.

Volume 41

21st Battalion The M.R. (*Erase heading not required.*) March, 1919.

Place	Date	Hour	Summary of Events and Information	Remarks and references to Appendices
Cassel	1.		In billets. Training & fatigues. Wet.	
do	2.		do do Wet.	
do	3.		do do do	
do	4.		do do Fair.	
do	5.		do do do	
do	6.		do do Wet.	
do	7.		do do do	
do	8.		do do Changeable.	
do	9.		do do do	
do	10.		do do do	
do	11.		do do Fair.	
do	12.		do do do	
do	13.		do do Blowery.	
do	14.		do do Fair.	
do	15.		do do do	
do	16.		do do do	
do	17.		do do Wet.	
do	18.		do do Fair.	
do	19.		do do do	
do	20.		do House M.Ed. Snow & Rain.	
do	21.		do do Fair.	
do	22.		do Musketry. do	
do	23.		do do do	
do	24.		do do do	
do	25.		do do do	
do	26.		do Reduced to Cadre Strength. 6 Officers & 217 Other Ranks transferred to 1/5th Battalion The Border Regt. Fair.	
do	27.		do Cleaning up. do	
do	28.		do do Snow.	
do	29.		do do Fine.	
do	30.		do Fair.	
do	31.		do	

LIEUT.-COLONEL
Chadwick
COMMANDING 21st BN. THE MANCHESTER REGIMENT.

List of Casualties for the Month of March.

1. Other Rank.   Injured   17/3/19.

List of Reinforcements for the Month of March.

2. Other Ranks.   Transfered from P.M.B.   14/3/19.

Army Form C. 2118.

WAR DIARY
or
INTELLIGENCE SUMMARY.

(Erase heading not required.)

Instructions regarding War Diaries and Intelligence Summaries are contained in F. S. Regs., Part II. and the Staff Manual respectively. Title pages will be prepared in manuscript.

Place	Date	Hour	Summary of Events and Information	Remarks and references to Appendices

Reinforcements for the Month of April, 1919.

Nil.

Casualties for the Month of April, 1919.

Army Form C. 2118.

21 Manchester V8 35

WAR DIARY
or
INTELLIGENCE SUMMARY.
(Erase heading not required.)

Instructions regarding War Diaries and Intelligence Summaries are contained in F. S. Regs., Part II. and the Staff Manual respectively. Title pages will be prepared in manuscript.

Place	Date	Hour	Summary of Events and Information	Remarks and references to Appendices

Andrews LIEUT.-COLONEL,
COMMANDING 21st BN. THE MANCHESTER REGIMENT.

WAR DIARY
or
INTELLIGENCE SUMMARY.

Army Form C. 2118.

(Erase heading not required.)

Army Form C. 2118.

WAR DIARY
or
INTELLIGENCE SUMMARY.
(Erase heading not required)

Volume #5.
21st Bn. Manchester Regiment July 1919.

Place	Date	Hour	Summary of Events and Information	Remarks and references to Appendices
Cambrai	1		In Billets. Showery	
do.	2		do. Fair	
do.	3		do. do.	
do.	4		do. do.	
En route	5		Entrained Cambrai. Arrived Etaples at 1000 hrs.	
LE HAVRE	6		Arrived LE HAVRE 14.00 hrs and taken up in No. 2 Rest Camp. Fair	
do.	7		In Rotunda No. 2 Rest Camp. Fair	
do.	8		do. do.	
do.	9		do. do.	9/7/19 11 3 Censored
do.	10		do. do.	
do.	11		do. do.	
do.	12		do. do.	
do.	13		do. do.	
do.	14		do. do.	
do.	15		do. do. Showery	
do.	16		do. do.	
do.	17		do. do. Fair	
do.	18		do. do.	
do.	19		do. do.	
do.	20		do. do. Showery	
do.	21		do. do. do.	
do.	22		Embarkment of WAR VARS. Fair 14/5 hrs.	
do.	23		Embarked troops for CAESAREA. Fair 14/5 hrs.	

Commanding 21st Bn. The Manchester Regiment.

www.ingramcontent.com/pod-product-compliance
Lightning Source LLC
Chambersburg PA
CBHW081548160426
43191CB00011B/1869